# Your Guided Hunt
## & What You Should Know

by
## Randy Blackburn

2014 - Tips
17% - 20%

*Cover and live animal Photographs*
Bob Hamilton

*Illustrations*
Randy Blackburn

All Rights Reserved
© 1996, Randy Blackburn
84 Southfork Road
Cody, Wyoming 82414

*Book and Cover Design*
Yellowstone Printing, Cody, Wyoming

ISBN 0-9654123-0-X

*~ This book is dedicated to my father who taught me how to ride and how to shoot, and so much more. And to my loving wife, Carole, who has patiently lived with the consequences.*

## Acknowledgments

I want to thank all the other guides who I have learned from, and the outfitters who have hired me. I want to thank all the hunters I have met who have helped me too. None of us learned it all on our own.

# Table of Contents

**Foreword** ................................................................... vii

**Introduction** ............................................................... ix

*Chapter I*
**Elk** ........................................................................... 1

*Chapter II*
**Booking the Hunt** ..................................................... 21

*Chapter III*
**Guide and Hunter** .................................................... 27

*Chapter IV*
**Shoot, Shoot, Shoot** ................................................ 39

*Chapter V*
**The Horseback Hunt** ............................................... 51

*Chapter VI*
**Trophy Care and Getting It Home** ........................... 65

*Chapter VII*
**Being Prepared** ....................................................... 75

*Chapter VIII*
**Some Hunting Tricks That Work** .............................. 89

*Chapter IX*
**Hunting Ethics** ........................................................ 101

*Chapter X*
**Dangerous Game** .................................................... 113

## Foreword

There is nothing more fascinating than the game we hunt. The animals live their lives in wild places enduring all that nature dishes out. Hunting allows us to become a real part of it all. It would have been nice to cover more details about the habits of the game animals, but I think it best to keep to the hunt for now.

The hunt. We call it sport for lack of a better term and most everyone agrees that it is much more than that. We choose to maintain a degree of difficulty in honor of the animal. Fair chase may well be the single most important ingredient.

I once heard someone say that it would be great if we could figure out a way to catch and release our game as some fishermen do. I'm not so sure. Killing is no less a part of the big picture than say, birth. Generally speaking most hunters are better at hunting the animals than photographers. Compared to hunters, photographers seldom put themselves through the blood, sweat, and tears as do hunters. When you say the word "hunter" everyone who hears knows exactly what you mean.

There are those who would like our term for ourselves to become a derogatory one. An attempt to cloud the truth in this manner only reminds us of what we already know. We are moving farther and farther from the land. How do you explain it?

I won't. I'll leave the explaining to someone better suited. What I will explain in these pages is the realness of it all. The triumphs, the blunders, the work, and the fun of hunting are the only things I want to convey. The "how to" parts of the book are only there to allow you to see what happens on a guided hunt just in case you have not been on one.

Much has been written from a hunter's perspective. I am a hunter of course, but by seeing the hunt from the guide's point of view I hope you will possibly see things differently. I have discussed many of the points in the book with other guides and outfitters. For the most part they agree. Your mechanic probably sees your automobile differently than you do, for instance.

In any event I hope you, the reader/hunter, can get something valuable from the book. I hope you finally go on that guided hunt you have been dreaming about.

*Randy Blackburn*

## Introduction

Most hunters dream of heading off to some wild place to hunt game that cannot be found in their own back 40. I think it is fair to say that Teddy Roosevelt allowed the idea of the guided hunt to become reality for the modern hunter. As a result one can readily find a quality guided and outfitted hunt in any remote corner of the globe.

This book may give you some insight as to what you might expect on such a hunt. Although this piece is written with the first timer in mind, I believe seasoned travellers and young guides could find something here of worth. The nuts and bolts of the hunt may remove some of the mystique. I hope the details answer many of your questions, or even prompt you into asking some more.

I must apologize for using so much of the first person, however I want you to know that this is firsthand information gleaned from 16 years of guiding hunters. I have not guided all over the world, but much of what you will find here can be applied anywhere you choose to hunt.

The hunting services that are out there for you are better today than ever. Outfitters and guides now have a history from which they can draw their expertise. A competitive market place has weeded out the less than quality outfits available to you. Your guided hunt is important to you, and this book can help you get the most out of it.

I am not currently in the outfitting business these days. I am a licensed and active guide. That means I am an employee doing what I do best. I am not selling hunts for anyone in the business, and I am not promoting any particular place. The stories center around the Rocky Mountain West only because that is where I guide.

The stories are real, though I have changed the names as you might guess. The trials and tribulations are a normal aspect of hunting, as are the successes and the good times. I hope you can feel the cold and taste the coffee. Perhaps you will sense the fellowship that combines the guide and hunter.

If, by reading this book, you decide to take action and book your hunt I will have done my part. You owe it to yourself to simply go. Good Luck!

*Randy Blackburn*

*Your Guided Hunt & What You Should Know*

# Elk
*Chapter I*

Rob's bull lay still on the steep slope. This particular hunt had been a tough one until Rob touched off a 300 yard shot to drop this elk cleanly right in his tracks. It had been a long hike from our vantage point on the opposite hillside just to get to the bull on this side. Happy hunter and guide, Rob and I found ourselves with only minutes of daylight remaining.

It was the second week of October. Low clouds covered the mountain tops as another Wyoming snow squall was gearing up into a full fledged storm. It was a good bull that now lay before us. Five points on the right horn (we still call them horns) and six on the left. The rack had no broken points and I quickly guessed his spread at 40 inches using Rob's 26 inch rifle barrel as a yard stick.

I fumbled with Rob's camera as he filled out his elk tag. His eyeglasses fogged over and ice started forming on my mustache. We hurriedly got the necessary pictures in a series of little blue flashes. Wind now whipped snowflakes into stinging projectiles. We were out in the center of a small meadow surrounded by timber, and although the trees could have afforded us some shelter. We couldn't drag the bull uphill. To slide the bull downhill into a pile of rocks, I knew, could result in breaking off one of the points.

Jubilant and freezing, Rob held onto the bull as I started to work. Using my knife I made an incision between the ears right on down the spine to the base of the tail. Next I made a ringing cut around the bull well behind the shoulders followed by another cut down from the center of each foreleg on the backside to the ringed cut leaving the brisket hide intact. The cape was then skinned up to the base of the skull. Using my belt hatchet I severed the base from the spine leaving a cape with head yet to be skinned.

Snow covered the ground now, giving us a little light to work by, and darkness settled in as I cut the bull into quarters. I left the spine, ribs, and belly hide attached with the entrails still inside this natural package. This method not only saves time by eliminating the gutting process, it also keeps the gut smell from getting out on the wind, thus attracting grizzlies to the kill site. Rob was shivering as I wrapped the back straps and neck fillets into the cape. I glanced around to make sure we didn't leave something the snow might cover up by morning.

Rob shouldered his rifle and drug the cape downhill. I drug one hind quarter in each hand leaving the two front quarters at the kill site. Halfway down I dropped off one hind quarter. When we hit bottom I piled the trim meat onto the remaining hind quarter. By spreading out the pieces I knew that a grizzly might find part of the kill and take it. It was unlikely however, that he would gather up all the pieces and claim them as would be the case if the entire elk was intact. There were no trees suitable for hanging anything let alone all this meat. I shouldered the cape with head attached, and Rob and I commenced the climb back to our saddle horses that were tied about a half a mile away.

By the time we hit the ridge top we were wet from perspiration and snow. We trudged along in the darkness, heads down with the wind at our backs. The horses knickered as we almost walked by them. I threw the cape down as my shoulders were burning from the weight. The horses were anxious to get back to camp as were we, but we were exhausted and half frozen.

I instructed Rob to get some sticks gathered up. He leaned his rifle against a nearby tree. We were too tired to talk. He assumed correctly that we were going to build a fire and he set about breaking off dry limbs. I kicked the snow away on the sheltered side of a large rock and slowly the little flame came to life. Rob came back with a good arm load that we soon had roaring.

Rob leaned back against the rock in the firelight. The flames flickered and I watched him for a moment, his orange hat and ear lugs pulled down to his chin. His shirt and coat were opened near the neck to let some of the steam out. His fogged over glasses rested on his knee, but otherwise he did have the look of your typical happy hunter.

"Randy, this is the toughest hunt I've ever been on." Rob said with eyes closed, and his head leaning back against the rock.

"Yea, it gets like this sometimes, but you got your bull." I answered.

"Yea. Right now I'm just dreaming about that shot. What a shot," He drifted off.

"Well don't fall asleep yet, we still have some stuff to do."

"What?"

"I've gotta finish caping out this bull. You shove some snow into this tin cup for tea and dry out some of our clothes while I'm caping."

Rob was one of those hunters who guides love to guide. He went right to work on both projects as I pulled the head and cape up near the fire for light. He was, it is true, a middle aged guy from Cincinnati. At this point in time though, we were both hunters of the Rocky Mountains. Friends toughing out the situation together.

The thought of camp and a warm supper began to gnaw at us. I hung the rack in a nearby pine with my lariat. I tied the cape across the back of my saddle then bridled the horses for the two mile ride back to camp. Rob kicked plenty of snow on the fire tramping it down again and again. The horses were more than ready and we struggled getting Rob aboard while his horse fidgeted.

The clouds were breaking up and the wind diminished. Stars twinkled above as the nighttime temperatures plummeted. The new snowfall accumulated on the pine boughs falling on my lap every time my horse brushed near one. Rob mentioned that his scabbard filled up with snow because the snap had come undone. I guess I was too miserable to care, or figured we didn't need the rifle anyway. I didn't reply.

We rode single file around the last bend in the trail toward camp. The smell of wood smoke hit me first, then the sight of the illuminated wall tents. I knew that supper had come and gone. The other guides and hunters would be waiting up for us assuming, and rightly so, that we got on a bull just before dark. The wrangle horse was picketed near the trail and he knickered as we rode in.

Jim and Ted came out of the dining tent to help us. After a few jokes about our frozen state they helped me with my mounts. The other hunters filed out to meet Rob. They all fell back into the tent to hear his story. Jim fed the horses while Ted and I lugged the saddles into the tack tent. I gave them a quick run down wanting to waste no time on my way to a warm tent and hot meal.

Katie, the cook, fixed us up in no time. The hunters headed off after the story of Rob's bull to their own tents. I knew Rob would have no trouble sleeping, dreaming about this day. Sitting next to the wood stove, we guides had plans to make for the morning. The next day would be the last day of the hunt. We would have to pack up the five hunters and head for home.

"Well," I said hugging a cup of coffee, "I have to go get that bull in the morning. It's gonna take awhile, so maybe I can hook up with you guys on the way out."

Ted grinned, "Yea, it's always a bitch goin' after a bull the morning ya have to pack out. I 'spose we can manage without you though."

We all understood the job. Come morning we would gather and saddle 21 head of saddle and pack animals for the trip out. Our wrangler, Tracy, was already asleep in the guide tent. He had to be the first up in the morning to wrangle the horses before any of the rest of us could get anything done.

It had been a good seven day hunt. From our wilderness camp we took three bulls. Each of Jim's hunters scored on respectable bulls. Ted's one hunter drew a blank. He passed up a good bull early on only to go without as it turned out. Rob got the biggest bull, though my other hunter, William, kind of pooped out at the end of the hunt. There would be one day off between hunts then the last hunt of the season would begin. Such is elk hunting.

Breakfast was catch as catch can. Supplies were running low by the end of the hunt. The gas lantern hissed in the dining tent as we all relived the week. The hunters were a happy bunch. Somehow they all looked much more seasoned than the day they rode in. Katie had to shop for groceries the next day. Tracy was yearning for a night in down, and we three guides were simply thinking about a warm couch for a day.

William might have been feeling a little desperate when he asked to go along with me to get Rob's bull. Rob had already offered to help. He was good help too, but William didn't have an elk and I was his guide. There was an outside chance we might see something while going after the downed bull. I really prefer to go back after a bull alone just in case a grizzly has claimed it, but William had that look.

Everyone was busy packing up for the trip out. William handed his duffel to Jim, and we headed out with our two saddle horses and two empty pack horses for the bull. I felt guilty about leaving the lion's share of the work to the others. Rob was standing under the meat pole admiring his cape with no horns. I gave him  the sign, and he hollered back that he would be waiting at the trailhead. Ted threw a snowball at my horse's butt, causing him to just about jump out from under me.

William and I turned off the main trail following my tracks of the night before. Our horses chugged up the mountain, their breath puffing like locomotives. It was getting on in the morning and I really doubted that we would see any elk. William was hopeful even though he chose not to hunt hard with us during the week. The sun was in my eyes and a glare came off the snow. That is probably why I didn't see the tracks sooner.

Abruptly, I checked my horse to a stop. The two pack horses piled up behind me. Bringing up the rear, William caught on to the commotion. The elk tracks were crossing my old trail at a ninety degree angle and pointing off to the next valley on our left.

"What's up?" William asked in a louder voice than necessary.

"Two elk crossed here real early this morning. From the size of these I think it's two bulls runnin' together."

"Where are they now?"

I motioned William up with a wave so we could talk without shouting. He rode up along side and I pointed my gloved finger along the tracks down the hill, and in the direction of the heavy timber on the opposite hill about a half mile away.

William looked over toward the timber and nodded.

"We could tie up here and hike over and see if we could find 'em."

"Maybe," I replied with some hesitation.

Well here it was staring me right in the face. I had to get Rob's bull out and to the trailhead 16 miles away. If we did get lucky and William should knock one down I only had enough pack horses for one bull. Dick, the outfitter and my boss, would be waiting at the trailhead to take all the hunters and their game to town. The hunters would have to check into their rooms and get meat to the butcher for their flights home. I could see this schedule didn't allow for overlap into the next hunt whereupon we would all have new obligations.

I thought for a moment about the possibility of Dick coming back for the elk, but he ran two separate camps and I knew he had more than enough to do getting both groups of hunters out and two new groups in. I added it up. Sixteen miles out. Forty miles to town with Rob's bull and forty back to the trailhead. Sixteen miles back in and out on these same horses, then 40 back into town. Even if the stock held out it would take two days. I felt selfish when thinking of my day off, but the fact of the matter is every guide wants to hunt right down to the marrow of his bones. Sometimes I believe I want the hunter to score more than he does. Still, the logistics had to be addressed.

"William, Rob's plane goes out the day after tomorrow, How 'bout you?"

"I gotta be at the airport at 5:30 tomorrow morning."

Slowly, it came to William what I was getting at. He kind of gave a relenting sigh.

"Your right. It's too late to go off after those elk. What would we do if I got one? Boy I wish this would have happened a couple a days ago."

Holding my hand near the brim of my hat from the glare, I squinted off toward the timber. Those elk were probably bedded on the steep side hill. Yet I knew they would spot us if we worked our way up to them.

"Okay, let's get Rob's bull and head for home."

I glassed the scene of the kill from where Rob made the shot. William marveled at the distance. I couldn't spot any tracks of bears or otherwise. To play it safe I rolled a basketball size rock down into the creek bottom. The crashing noises would flush a bear if one had claimed the hind quarter down in the timber.

"No bear. Good deal. William, let's go down and pack this bull. We'll pick up the horns on the way back."

We hit the main trail around noon. I had the pack horses in tow with William following behind. The sun warmed things up to a comfortable state, and we gabbed back and forth about the mountains. It's funny, but during the hunt you keep quiet because your hunting, and as a result we found plenty to talk about on the way out. Katie had packed our lunches and we nibbled at lunch from our saddle bags as we rode. William shot what seemed like a whole roll of film at Rob's bull being packed. From the tracks I guessed our party to be about an hour in front of us.

It was late in the afternoon as we rode into the trailhead. Our guys were still unpacking as was the other outfit that came out from 10 miles the other direction. Their three hunters had scored on one bull, a big one. Glancing at the rack laying by the outfitters truck I figured around three fifty gross score. William tied up and walked over to the mountain of gear to find his duffel. I threw in unpacking with the others as Tracy the wrangler was engaged in a friendly dispute with the wrangler from the other outfit.

"Well, we got three for five and you guys only got one for three." Tracy said as he lugged another kitchen pannier toward the pile.

"Yea, but we got the biggest bull. Ya can see that," replied the other wrangler.

They were stripping pack saddles bantering back and forth when the other wrangler asked me.

"Randy, what do you think?"

"Ah, I don't know, why don't you add up all the points on all the horns and divide by the number of hunters. Then see which camp has the most points."

They each gave me that look as if to say "Why did we bother asking you anyway?" Then they went right on arguing about it.

Dick had a little pow wow with we three guides covering the last hunt and some points about the next hunt. He had been in three days earlier, working both his camps simultaneously to keep all ends running smoothly. Dick was a good man to work for. He understood the game, treating all of his hunters and hands fairly. He would take the hunters and their elk to town while we hauled everything else back to his place for repacking between hunts. Katie and Julia, the camp cook from the other camp, were going over grocery lists on the hood of Dick's pickup.

It had been a good hunt. Hunters and guides from both camps mingled and laughed recalling good times. Even those who were going home without an elk were unanimous in saying they had a great wilderness hunt. Dick and the wranglers were about loaded up, and we all promised to meet in town later than night. Our hunters tipped us well. Tracy came out ahead acquiring a brand new sleeping bag from one of Jim's hunters. They handed Katie an envelope and each hunter hugged her before climbing into the vehicles for the trip to town.

To coin an old Las Vegas phrase, "The faces change, but the game stays the same." That is true, however in this game many of the friendships made are enduring. Hunters and guides have a bond that goes far beyond that of a cabbie and his fare. When you live together for a week or more in the wilderness people learn or relearn the necessity of working with other people. Gone are the distractions of the workplace and most civilized aspects as we know them. The goal of bagging an elk includes the help of the wrangler and the cook for instance. Even after years of guiding and outfitting I find it amazing at what lengths we will go to to hunt elk, or other game for that matter.

The lonely Crow warrior sat by the wallow. Teddy Roosevelt traveled along in a caravan that hunted for months on end. And today, we have refined various tactics to hunt elk that have each more or less become a sport unto itself.

The act of hunting elk is really broken down to which style of elk hunting are we going to pursue. Style might also be broken down into scientific regional classifications.

On the other hand I would choose to deal with types like private land elk. Migrating or free ranging elk are another consideration. Some elk live high in the elevations most of the year, while some range around the foothills or river bottoms. Elk in a dense population too, will act differently sometimes as compared to elk found only sparsely throughout their range.

It is your guide who knows these variables, and it is he who should be able to draw from a bag of tricks to put the hunter in the best possible situation to bag a bull. A guide and hunter who work in sync will assuredly increase their chances.

September will, in most cases, kick off the elk season. Some states will offer rifle or muzzle loader hunts, though most states throughout the Rocky Mountain area will open their archery seasons in the month of September. The bulls will have rubbed the velvet from their antlers in the latter part of August, but the rut will not get well underway until the middle of September.

In early September bulls are feeling the first effects of the rut. They rub their antlers attacking various trees and sometimes even sagebrush. A limited amount of bugling will occur in the morning and evening. Bulls will use wallows at this time of year, and this key is a good one for unlocking success.

A wallow is a mud hole in which the bull elk rolls in to plaster himself with mud and his own urine. As unpleasant as this might seem it makes him attractive to females and actually cools him off as he becomes agitated, and "hot" just before and during the rut. In dry country I have found where bulls will wallow on dusty ground after urinating on it. When a seep or bog is in the neighborhood though they do prefer this.

In the vicinity of the wallow the trees will be rubbed identifying another of the bulls' methods of marking his territory. Mud will often be splattered high up on nearby trees as a result of the bull shaking the mud off his coat similar to a dog shaking off water. The stench around a heavily used wallow often reveals the location before you see it. In higher elevations bulls tend to wallow more in the daylight than they do at night for a very logical reason. Nighttime temperatures make the water too cold to roll in comfortably. In the 70 or 80 degree heat of midday this same wallow has a soothing effect on the bull

In my bag of tricks I use several useful tactics to increase the odds of a shot. I like to position bow hunters in a tree well within bow range of the wallow. Rifle hunters can build a blind a good distance away, always keeping the wind in mind. If time permits a couple of blinds might be needed for wind changes. If the bull becomes spooked from one blind he can be hunted from another at the same wallow.

If two or more wallows are found in a small area of the same bog I throw logs across all but one of the wallows. This forces the bull to use the one I want him to. Then too, I sometimes stick a small twig in various wallows to see which ones are being hit on a regular basis. Muddy water or lack thereof doesn't always tell the truth. Some water settles quickly while other wallows will remain muddy with no use for days.

We once took a bull with a bow at such a place. The hunter was up in a leaning pine at 18 yards from our wallow. I was up another tree about twenty yards to his right. The six point bull came in slow looking all around. He walked up and sniffed, then pawed at the mud at the water's edge. I figured the hunter would shoot soon, but the bull was quartering toward him and I knew he wanted a broadside, or quartering away shot. The bull went down before either of us expected any of this. We looked at each other with only the whites of or eyes showing under the face paint. The bull was on his back thrashing around throwing all of the water right out of the bog. Suddenly it occurred to me that this was a great shot. If the hunter could put an arrow right into his ribs from the bull's bottom side it would leave a perfect blood trail. Luckily my hunter thought the same thing. The arrow slipped silently into the bull just ahead of the diaphragm and into both lungs as it turned out.

The bull had one horn hooked under a root for a second then struggled to his feet. He looked around for another second or two much the way he did when he came in. He jumped out of the mud then trotted off. Soon he was walking with his head held kind of low, then he simply fell over. This happened while we watched. No tracking was necessary which is quite unusual in the bow hunting game.

At the time neither myself or the hunter had ever heard of anyone shooting into the bottom side of an elk. To this day it's the only time I've seen it.

The rut is undoubtedly the most exciting time to hunt elk. It is the classic elk hunt. Calling bulls on frosty Indian summer mornings or shadowy golden evenings is the stuff calenders are made of. Elk are more vulnerable at this time and as a result many areas are cutting back on rifle seasons at this time. Though the elk seem vulnerable it can be a complex type of elk hunting. Like bear baiting it is not a lead pipe cinch.

Mid-September will spark the rut. It may vary a little from region to region or from year to year. Bulls become more vocal and a great shuffle and reshuffle of territories takes place. Gathering and holding harems of cows is the first order of business for the bulls. It is a frenzied time in areas of medium and high populations, but a bit more subtle in areas with a low count.

The typical scenario has the guide bugling to locate a bull. If he gets an answer he and the hunter try to cut off some of the distance and set up to cow call the bull into range. This tried and true method is much the same as turkey hunting in the spring of the year. It's those damndable variables that always come into play just when you thought it was easy.

The bull that was regularly using his wallow and grazing in the same meadow at night has now changed his habits drastically almost overnight. He's on the move keeping his cows, or gathering more. Rival bulls threaten him, and he has to bed higher or in dark jungles to protect what's his. If the bull has no cows of his own he will wander to and fro looking for an opportunity making him hard to pattern if your only reading the sign. Small bulls will hang on the outskirts of a herd traveling with, but not really with them. These satellite bulls, as they are called, are not always small but these bulls make up the biggest portion of the available bulls in a given range.

Basically you have three types of personalities during the rut. Herd bulls are dominant and usually large. Wanderers can be of any size, but are solitary creatures roving about challenging various herd bulls for their cows. Lastly, the satellite bulls may hang around a particular herd hoping for their chance. It isn't uncommon to have several satellite bulls around a good sized herd of cows. The more cows the more scent they give off to attract males.

As stated previously there are times that all of this activity seems absent during the rut. This is the case in areas of low elk populations. In this instance bulls can breed at leisure, or at least without constant challenges from numerous other bulls. These bulls are not nearly as vocal. They are more apt to run from a bugle than they are to respond to it. Cow calling works as always, but even here the bulls act timid or wary.

Weather plays a roll too. Bright sunny high pressure systems get the bulls going. Rainy days, or worse yet, snow storms, cause them to more or less shut down for the duration. Likewise, I find that the dark of the moon creates more day time activity. Some would argue this of course, but it has been my observation.

Everyone wants a big bull. A big anything though isn't easy. Herd bulls are obviously smarter because they are older. The concentration of cows makes it much more difficult to call the bull away when you're sounding like one lone cow. Then again, all those sets of cow eyes on you makes it tremendously hard for the guide and hunter to go undetected. One alarm bark from an old cow quickly sends the entire herd off.

Nevertheless, this is still the best hunt. Perhaps with the exception of a migration, you should see more bulls on a rut hunt than a wallow hunt or post rut hunt.

I prefer to ride or walk along in the dark of the morning. Bugling with a few coughs and grunts will generally get a response. If my hunter can do a reasonable job of calling I have him bugle as well, imitating two bulls. We pick the one that either sounds mature, or the one that is the closest to us. Bulls do not all sound the same and you cannot always estimate the size of a bull from his bugle. I file away the locations of these bulls in my mind for later in the morning should our first plan go sour.

After tying up the horses we head off as silently as we can to cut the distance between us and the bull. If you're not careful at this point you can run right into them in the dark and ruin what was started. The bull may even be working his way toward you. In the gray of the morning I let out a spike bull squeal or a chuckle to test the waters as it were. If the plan is working the bulls should answer from somewhere in the vicinity.

The fun really gets rolling at this point. If I am guiding one or two bow hunters, I set them up right where we are, then I move back 40 yards or so to continue to call. I will say right here that I don't mind guiding two bow hunters as the bull will come in on one side or the other. These weapons are short range, and the hunters are not competing with each other because they simply can't shoot far, especially in thick cover. I don't want the hunter to call in this case as the bull will hone in on the position giving the hunter away. When rifle hunting I sit with the shooter and we both call. At this point we are cow calling to imitate a stray cow or cows. Remember this is similar to turkey hunting, and we are trying to sound like hens being stolen by a lesser tom.

My favorite bull is the wanderer. He is generally a mature animal but for whatever reason he doesn't gather a harem. His style is solitary and he moves from harem to harem hoping for the best. Satellite bulls are also easy to call although they are not generally trophy size. It happens that a satellite bull could be a decent six, but it doesn't happen often.

The most difficult bull to call into range is the herd bull. He has his harem and he isn't often in the mood to go running off on a hunch when he has a bunch of sure things to watch over. Rifle hunters have a much better chance at a herd bull simply because they are able to shoot farther. If I can get a herd bull just to come out and give us a look the chances are good we can take him.

In the country I guide in I figure I need five bulls to call one into archery range. Changing wind, mistakes on our part, and bad luck all take a toll. While rifle hunting I assume I'll need three bulls to get in shooting range of one for the same reasons. The time of the rut also changes these figures somewhat. Hunting pressure also wises bulls up so to speak, making it tougher to be successful.

When a bull comes in to a call it is suffice to say that his ears brought him in. He recognizes familiar sounds that trigger a response. He hears elk. Foreign noises such as talking, or bolts racking in a round will spook him. Then again a cracking twig may or may not alarm him. After all real elk crack twigs all the time. At times I will even rake the brush with a stick to simulate a bull thrashing about. It depends upon what mood I perceive the bull to be in. Bow hunters must remain particularly quiet as I want the bull to pass right by them as he comes into my call.

The bull wants to see something as he gets in close. Their eyesight is very good. He is wanting to see a cow or the little bull that is giving him fits. One unorthodox trick is to use a small elk antler tauntingly moving just behind a tree or bush. An elk truly does know what a horn is when he sees it. A big part of a bull's life revolves around his horns and those horns of other bulls. A small antler is not very threatening and a large antler is a pain to pack around all day while you're hunting.

A tan piece of canvas or buckskin works too. If the caller is positioned behind the shooter the caller can show this tan piece in a hide and seek fashion to the bull. Elk are tan in color. He thinks he's watching this elk move through the timber. Yes, elk are color blind and another color may work. I feel though that since elk are tan it makes me feel better about using that color. Other hunters are apt not to use these tactics and as a result this has worked for me especially in heavily hunted country.

The other sense you have to accommodate is the sense of smell. I have used strips of bull elk belly hide with the sticky urine on it too help fool bulls. Cow elk urine also helps. Wallow mud or elk droppings also give off elk smell and can be placed on a rag or ground into your clothing if your in a hurry. These smells will attract elk, but do not count on smells to cover up your own human scent. After trying various sprays and soaps I am convinced that one cannot cover up your scent from the approaching elk if the wind is wrong. If the wind is right, it's right. If the wind is wrong the bull will smell you in spite of anything you try.

Elk depend on their sense of smell as much as any wild animal. You can be sure of that. Bulls will often circle to get downwind of your position. They will do this if you let them. The trick is to get the shot before he gets around you. A small piece of frayed yarn on your rifle or bow can be used as a wind indicator. I rely on a small plastic bottle filled with flour to check the wind direction. I just squeeze the bottle and the flour puffs out of the small squirt-type opening. This method detects even the most subtle of wind currents.

Mornings aren't the only time bulls respond to calling. Some may even argue that evenings are best. Most old time outfitters and guides traditionally hunted only the evening hunt. The reason for this was that the elk were not pressured with a morning and evening hunt, so they hung around without leaving for parts unknown. In cases of heavy hunting pressure elk will either leave the country or become almost totally nocturnal.

As elk get up from their day beds they are relaxed and ready to feed. Instinctively they know that nighttime is coming and they feel safe. Today's elk know full well that man runs around in the daylight. When you call a bull in this situation he may not become immediately hot, but he is more apt to be curious, thus responding to you only a little more slowly.

Morning elk may have been running and fighting all night to protect or gain cows. If this has occurred a bull might be shy of calls. He may answer while leaving you trying to keep up with his retreat. A tough night of rutting can make for a bull that just wants to go home and go to bed.

Unfortunately hunting can be competitive these days. Other hunters try to outdo each other. Riding up and down the trail bugling all day only wises up the bulls to the fact that something is wrong here. Desperate acts by hunters does not produce bulls desperate to get shot at.

I hunt both morning and evening as it is the times we live in. If I had a choice, say on large tracts of private land, I would hunt only in the evening. This will allow plenty of quality hunting while it also keeps the elk naive to the fact that hunting season is going on.

Old time hunts used to last for 10 days or two weeks. Today's hunters can only get away from their responsibilities for shorter periods of time. The length of hunting season has been cut back in most states also. To stay in business the outfitter must book enough hunts to make it work. In essence, shorter hunts and seasons are a fact of life that causes us all to work the animals with more intensity than used to be the case.

I do draw the line at midday. By running into the bedding timber at this time only spooks the elk well away from their evening hangout. Midday hunting almost always ruins the evening hunt. Midday can be spent quietly scouting for sign or resting yourself. In September the days are still quite long. If your up well before dawn and get to bed late after the evening hunt...well, you figure it out. Remember the elk are sleeping too at this time. The odd bull may not, but chances are good you won't even get an answer at midday.

By the first of October the rut is waning. Iced over wallows reminds one of an abandoned shack. Rubbed trees have that dry look of age. Calling can still produce, but each passing day now loses it's luster for this type of hunting. Bulls are still with the cows, and some bulls have even paired together calling a truce. A change in tactics may be needed and an experienced guide knows when to adjust.

Mid-October calls for the old glass and stalk game. The waiting game of sitting by the trail isn't romantic, but necessary. Feed is the priority. Feed is the key. The winter migration is still far off, and the rut is over. It is the toughest of elk hunting. That's why they put the season there. Ironically enough this is the time most of the elk are harvested.

In the early morning you try to get to the elk meadow while they are still out and feeding. As daylight comes you may have an hour of open feeding but fifteen minutes is really more like it. The elk have been hunted and they are shy. They move into cover as if they were afraid of the daylight. If there is a bull in the bunch he'll most likely bring up the rear as usual. The bull will be the light colored one with darker legs and nearly black belly. A mature bull will be half again bigger than the cows and calves.

Should guide and hunter be in position there isn't much to it. In rugged terrain though, getting up to the meadow without being detected in the dark isn't easy. The elk will head for the thickest, steepest country to bed in. Any alarm just sends them there that much quicker. If the overall country isn't too thick however, another system can be employed.

By watching a herd of elk from a distance you can watch which way the elk go to bed. Sometimes you might get lucky enough to watch them bed. Using binoculars or a spotting scope you will be able to stay way back while the elk are at ease and acting naturally. From the vantage point you can now take your time and plot a stalk. The wind, lay of the land, etc., can be taken into account and guide and hunter are able to go over the pros and cons of various strategies. This is a good situation to be in. Through the glasses you will have already determined if there is a bull in the herd. In the gray of the morning it is often impossible to see antlers, but the bull's color (again lighter than cows) will give him away.

Rather than following tracks into the bed ground it is wiser to approach from the direction the elk were headed when they timbered up. The guide knows that they will be headed for the thickest stand of timber. Get above or beyond where the best country lies.

When I get into position to start the stalk I get my hunter right in front of me. I keep close enough to whisper directions or touch him on the shoulder to point out the elk, should I see them first. Quiet, deliberate stalking skills are needed at this point. Frankly speaking, hunting deer from a tree stand does nothing to sharpen these skills. Soft soled boots and silent clothing are needed to keep noise to the barest minimum. The hunter must swivel his head in all directions and he must be ready. The guide will steer the hunter around obstacles and keep the hunter pointed in the right direction.

While sneaking up on elk that you know are there, one must have a round in the chamber. Don't fall into the notion that slinging your rifle over your shoulder will work. Carry the rifle at port arms. If the elk spot you first, and they almost always do, get the gun up closer to your shoulder. If the guide and hunter are walking slowly and close together the elk often think you're both another four footed animal. They may get up slowly rather than bolt crashing down the mountain in pandemonium.

I carry a small cow elk call in my mouth as we stalk. When we spot elk I mew softly to keep them calm. It isn't that I'm calling elk in, it just allows the two of us to appear as one elk moving through the timber. Sometimes it works and sometimes it doesn't.

Eastern hunters are as a rule very adept at pointing shotguns as they use them more often than their rifles. Western hunters get more rifle handling it seems due to the fact that more rifle seasons are open for various types of big game. When hunting on my own I like to have my rifle scope cranked up to nine power. When I spot the bull I can pick out part of a horn. I can differentiate between the shoulder and the rump. In the timber you will only see pieces and parts of the elk. If the rifle scope is on say, four power, the magnification may not be enough to pick out the details.

Many hunters are not comfortable with this method because they haven't had the practice. On nine power the field of view is cut down and they wind up searching all over for the patch of fur they just saw with their naked eye. Valuable time is wasted in this waving of the gun barrel, and the bull runs off to freedom. Hence, practice before the hunt pays off big time. Throw your rifle up to your shoulder time and again until it seems to fall right on target as your shotgun does. One key to remember is to lay your trigger finger alongside the trigger guard. Slip your finger into the trigger guard when you intend to shoot. At least this little safety detail will keep a stray from prematurely flying off into the trees. It could also save a life if some terrible form of mistaken identity takes place.

The guide will probably recognize the bull first. Size and color again gives him away even before you spot the rack. Two or three bulls could result in confusion, but this is rare. Which bull to take does not happen as much as, "is this bull good enough to take?" Some elk hunting areas have legal point restrictions on the number of points on the rack. It may require a long look to make sure the bull is a legal bull. The guide is supposed to know his stuff. If he sees the legal number of points and says "Shoot" or "Take him" the hunter generally does just that. Some hunters will not take anyone's word for it and wait until they personally see the rack. This is a good policy. Even though an elk might get away without a shot fired, an illegal elk sure ruins a hunt quickly.

Most competent guides do know their stuff however. I have never had a bad experience along these lines, but I don't hunt in a point restrictive area. A guide can look at the brow tine or last fork of the horn and tell what kind of bull he's looking at. He might be off on the width of the rack or a broken point, but his guess at a glance will be very close to reality.

To be candid I have had hunters who have relied on my judgement, and I have had hunters who waited to see for themselves. Sometimes we waited too long and the elk was gone. It all goes back to the fact that this is hunting. There are many variables. The hunter/guide trust is a very important one. This all goes out the window in the case of charging, dangerous game. When the guide says shoot, you shoot.

It is still mid season and now mid day. In areas of large elk populations, hunter and guide might work various fingers of timber. Sometimes the guide even rolls a boulder down into the thick stuff to get them up and moving. You might even mount up and leave the present spot for another miles away. This gives you the time to get into position for the evening hunt.

If I am hunting a minimum population, or planning on spending the entire day in one area, I detest stirring up the elk in the middle of the day. Like the rutting season hunt, it spooks the elk and ruins the evening hunt. It is the evening ambush that has a far greater chance for success.

The sun goes over the mountain and the shadows get long. The temperature starts to fall and the wind dies down. This is the evening hunt. Elk slowly appear in grassy aspen patches or side hill meadows. A shot from a good solid rest almost always pays off. Rather than playing catch up in the morning or stalking later, you are in control. During the evening the elk are headed toward you and you are ready.

A symphony conductor keeps the musicians playing it over and over in hopes of finally getting it right. Guides are much the same. Day after day, and season after season, a guide figures that at some point, trial and error will give way to getting it right every time out. The elk however, are not as predictable as whitetail deer. Elk may feed in one meadow one evening and a creek bottom a mile and a half from there the next evening. Elk may come out early, thus saving you from a long wait on the cold ground, or they may come out an hour after dark. Even the evening hunt can draw a blank.

I look forward to the dark of the moon. I think, without being able to prove it, that elk come out earlier in the evening on a dark phase of the moon. The advent of a storm also helps. All game seems to be active before the storm. I guess game feels the need to stock up on feed just in case it's a bad one. Then too, post storm high pressure brings them out. It is as if they are happy to get out of the house after being cooped up. Stable, unchanging weather on bright moon nights seems to put elk hunting into the doldrums.

*When it all pays off!*

The migration hunt is not available everywhere elk are found, but it is a great hunt where elk leave the snow covered mountains for wintering grounds in the foothills. Sometimes large herds can be spotted on the move. All elk are heading in one direction. The elk you see today will be long gone by tomorrow. Fifty to 100 miles of elk trails that are generations old tell the story.

The migration hunt is the best chance for a trophy bull. It is also much more difficult to draw a license as this hunt has only a limited amount of licenses available in most states. I have shown hunters 40 or 50 bulls during the migration in the same country I could find only two or three during mid-October.

Private land hunts can really pay off here as much of the winter range is on ranch lands. Public land hunting is usually conducted on migration trails leading to the winter grounds. Old cows lead the way picking up more and more elk as they go. Bulls may travel together in bachelor groups though many just throw in with the cows. The old bulls are smart. They prefer to have large herds of cows and calves breaking trail for them through the deep snow.

This is cold weather hunting. Bitter cold early in the morning and evening should be expected. It is November or December in the Rockies and icy creek crossings and icy roads are the norm. The hunter needs so much clothing that hiking all around the countryside requires tremendous effort. Pickup trucks are generally used on the private land hunts, though foot or horseback travel is still necessary to get around in the mountains. Snowmobiles work well where they are allowed.

The elk have winter prime pelts at this time. A bull elk cape is much more impressive now than the same cape would have been in September. Since there is a good background of snow on the ground it is easier to judge antlers at a glance. The elk paw through the fresh snow to uncover grass below. These wash tub looking affairs will dot the hillside in areas of good feed.

Feeding areas along the migration route are good places to hunt. Each passing bunch of elk will pause here to feed as well. This is due to the fact that less pawing is required since previous herds did the work for them. I have watched large bulls push other elk out of these holes in the snow using their antlers to gouge lessor elk. Elk still move better early or late in the day, but this is one time that elk hunting can be good at any time of the day.

I like to set up well away from a trail that has some feed along it. Two or 300 yards is about right. This may seem like a long ways, I agree, but I have my reasons.

Air currents drift back and forth during the day. The farther I am from the trail the less likely it is for elk to scent us. Then too, 20 or 30 elk have a good chance of spotting you with that many eyes looking in all directions. It's nice to build a fire to keep warm when the thermometer dips. If I set up downwind with the prevailing wind, the hunter and I can keep warm on these long waits without being detected.

Two or 300 yards may appear quite far if your not used to shooting beyond one hundred yards, I agree. Today's firearms are more than capable of the task. A bull elk has 22 inches of good chest cavity without counting the hair on the edges. Many rifle calibers have less than five inches of drop at 300 yards when the rifle is sighted in at only 100 yards. These calibers are flat shooters. Calibers that might be considered real dogs might drop 15 inches at this range. From a good rest this type of shooting is certainly not out of the question. Hunters should not be intimidated by range. Doubt alone will make you miss. Confidence comes from shooting. Shoot at 200 and 300 yards at home before the hunt. Don't rely on sighting in at 100, figuring the math will compensate for the rest. The actual shooting gives you the practice needed to do the job. I advise elk hunters to sight in to be on at 200 yards with most calibers. Of course, I assume these rifles to have quality scopes mounted on them.

The argument over which caliber is best will go on forever. Yes, I've seen .243s kill elk. No, it is not my choice. I prefer larger calibers that push a bullet along at a good clip. Medium weight bullets are my choice over heavy rounds for most calibers simply because they retain the punch while still reaching out there with accuracy.

In the country I hunt a wounded elk can jump off into two days work in about 20 seconds. It has happened, believe me. The rifle caliber with real muscle behind it can anchor a bull right in his tracks or within a few feet of the same.

We have to live with the follow-up aspect in archery season, true. But look at it this way. Should a hunter hit a bull that is in the company of other elk, this is what happens. If he is still on his feet as the others take off he tries to follow. Now he is a moving target and much harder to hit. As the others leave he panics and jumps off into cover or over a steep side hill as his instincts tell him too. A second shot may not even be possible. The lone archery bull just kind of wanders off because he wasn't with the herd when he was called in, thus the herd may move off, but not under the panic of gunfire.

Our wounded bull can't keep up with the bunch, so he heads for cover quick. In gentle country this may not be a real concern, but it can spell trouble in the mountains. Hard hitting guns do not create the confusion of a hit or miss either. It can happen, but not usually. When all the elk take off you don't want to be asking yourself, "Now which one was it? Should I shoot again because I've missed?" Here again the guide is watching with an objective eye as the hunter is shooting. A guide can tell you more about your shot, or shots, than you will realize yourself.

Elk hunting is a tough game. It is a real sport. More hunters aspire to some day go on a guided elk hunt than any other type of guided hunt. In fact, more mule deer hunting is conducted on guided hunts than elk hunting because more licenses are issued. Bull elk, nevertheless, is the dream of almost all big game hunters.

# Booking the Hunt
## Chapter II

I owned a nice little outfitting business at the time. I have since sold out going back to guiding only, my long suit. It was February 1991 and I had a booth rented at the sport show in Pittsburgh. This was my first attempt at booking hunts at one of these shows, and I figured that since everyone else did it that way, it must be "the" way to book clientele.

I had a good spot nestled in amongst outfitters from Maine to Alaska. Here at his fingertips, a hunter could book any type of hunting trip or fishing trip that he ever dreamed of. There were literally thousands of perspective customers walking about helping themselves to all the brochures they could carry. In this steady drone of activity I couldn't miss. I was ready and willing to sell hunting trips for nine species of big game and turkeys. I had trout fishing trips and scenic summer trips as well. I had it made.

At weeks end I must have talked with several hundred hunters. I actually booked five bear hunters. They were all great guys who later came back to hunt deer and elk also. At the time I counted this as a disappointment. I did receive some good exposure that came in handy later on down the road, but I figured I would have checks sticking out from all my pockets. The long drive back to Wyoming gave me time to think it over.

Most people make their money the hard way. They earn it. Business and family obligations don't always allow for grand hunting trips. It was also no small thing that so many outfitters had so much to offer. This sliced the client pie into many little pieces. I had to realistically ask myself, "How is the hunter to choose?"

Actually there are many ways to find and book the hunt of your dreams. Magazine ads are a start. Word of mouth is very reliable. Booking agents and hunting consultants can be a great aid. Sport shows give you the face-to-face, one-on-one aspect, while videos entertain you. Hunting for your hunt resembles the real hunt in some ways. Patience is important. Recognizing a good thing when you find it helps too. Choosing a hunt can be as involved as you want it to be. I suggest you be discriminatory. Get what you want.

They are called outfitters, not the ones who sell sporting goods, but they are the people who conduct the hunt. In Alaska they may be called master guides. In Africa they may be called white hunters. Outfitters may own or lease private land on which to hunt, or they may operate on a host of various public lands. Some of course, operate on a combination of both. Outfitters own the business, set the prices, and provide the service. In some instances these are termed as guiding services.

Guides are employees of outfitters. Guides actually guide hunters in the field. Outfitters may also guide themselves, but let's face it, an outfitter has so many responsibilities, he may not be able to guide as much as you might think. The guides are the mechanics of the auto repair shop.

Booking agents are just what the name implies. They book hunts. These businesses have many outfitters in their stable so to speak. The booking agent handles all booking aspects for all types of outfitters. They know their outfitters personally, and have been to their camps. The booking agent handles hunt deposits, contracts, license application and so forth. They advertise widely, and the outfitter benefits from the booking agent's ads. As the middleman in this process the booking agent gets a percentage from the outfitter, not from you.

The term hunting consultant is really synonymous with booking agent. The same service applies. In fact, the term "hunting consultant" is out pacing the term booking agent. In either event you can expect that their outfitters have a good enough track record to be solicited by a hunting consultant. Some outfitters are quite capable of booking their own clientele. They may have the time and the salesmanship skills it takes. Some outfitters have a ranch to run in the winter. Some may be off mountain lion hunting or working shows. Others lack the skills to sell, but are very good woodsmen nevertheless. It runs the gamut.

I suggest a telephone call to the agent or the outfitter. Letters and faxes are okay, but an actual conversation allows you to ask all the questions you have on your mind and receive an immediate reply. Ask for all printed literature and price lists. Prices changes from year to year. Be clear in conveying that you want current information.

Recently much of this information can be found on the Internet or World Wide Web. Hunting consultants and outfitters may have this information on the screen after you pull them up. Study. Study everything very carefully. Are the prices competitive? Some prices may appear to be a bit more expensive because this is an exclusive private land, or Indian Reservation hunt. Other prices that appear too low may not provide all the services you are looking for. Don't get drop camps confused with guided hunts.

Recent trophy pictures tell an interesting story. These photos are almost always genuine. Sadly enough a small percentage of these "kill pictures" are borrowed, or worse, though this is rare. I always placed a great deal of emphasis on my hunters photos. Last year's kills led directly to this year's business.

After you boil it down to three or four you can move on to the next step. It's time to get references. Three or four names of recent hunters is all you will need. Try not to be concerned with only those people who bagged trophy animals. Not everyone scores for various reasons. It is helpful to talk with the hunter who did not pop a cap on game. If he believes he had a great hunt he'll tell all unabashedly. Hunters can give you insight from a hunter's point of view.

One must ascertain whether or not game is plentiful. Are conditions physically rigorous? Is the hunt conducted in an orderly fashion? Does everyone receive equal treatment? Are the guides capable? These are the high points. You may have more questions for the reference hunter, but this is the gist of it.

Once you have settled in on a particular outfitter it is time to ask for a booking contract. Read it over carefully. Hunt contracts are not nearly as complicated as they sound. There is a good reason for contracts though. It protects you and the outfitter. After all money is changing hands and this makes it a business agreement. Most states require a contract between client and outfitter. Licensed and permitted outfitters are held accountable to far more regulatory agencies than you would ever dream. If the outfitter you choose doesn't offer a contract it may be due to the fact that he is not a legal outfitter. The ramifications of this could leave you in a sorry state of affairs if you book the hunt anyway.

Outfitters, and guides for that matter, are licensed by the state or province they work in. If you have any doubts a quick call to the licensing agency will put your mind at rest.

If you like what you read in the contract it is now time to book the hunt by signing it, and sending along the required amount of deposit. You may be instructed to send along the amount of the license money to the state also. This will be over and above the cost of the hunt in most cases.

In some places an outfitter may have licenses available from the state. In other cases you may have to apply in a drawing. Lastly you may simply be able to purchase a license over the counter when you arrive to hunt. Allow the hunting consultant or outfitter to fill out and send the application for you. One small mistake could kick you right out of a computer draw. These folks to this for a living. They are familiar with the process, and they are not apt to make a mistake. Deadlines are important also. Your mail service may not get your license money to the state on time should you wait until the last minute. Again, the hunting consultant or outfitter will not let this happen. It would be a foolish way to lose business.

While we're on the subject of hunting licenses you may bear in mind that many states have gone to the point system on some species. Typically the point system applies to only those animals that are found in limited supply in a certain range. Desert bighorn sheep, bighorn sheep, Shiras moose, and Rocky Mountain goats are now commonly placed under the point system.

You get one point each year you apply for a license. These points accumulate at a rate of one paint a year. In some states your name goes into the draw one, two, or three times depending on the number of preference points you have built up. In this type of draw you will have that many chances to draw. In other types of point system draws you also accumulate points in the same manner. This time, however, the state may draw from say all the three point applicants first. If licenses are still available, they then draw from the two point applicants. You can see that first year, or one point applicants, have little or no chance to draw a license.

Don't be discouraged. It isn't like buying a deer license over the counter in your home state, that's for sure. The system does work well with a little patience. Like the lottery, you have to play to win.

A deposit for partial payment for prior to the hunt is necessary for several reasons. The deposit locks in your hunt dates. Other hunters are booking as well, and the early bird gets the worm. It also holds all parties to their word. The hunting season is short. If the hunter backs out at the last minute the outfitter cannot replace him on the spur of the moment. In the same vein, should an unscrupulous outfitter leave you standing at the airport, what are you to do?

*Drawing a sheep license isn't easy.*

A percentage of the outfitter's gross income for the commercial use of public land must be paid to the government body in charge, (U.S. Forest Service, Bureau of Land Management, and state land boards). The outfitter pays these fees well in advance of the hunt. This amount is figured into the hunt, not added on. The liability insurance that is required to operate is also a big expense early in the calender year, long before the hunting season comes around. These, and other costs, make it necessary for a deposit to be required.

Most good hunting contracts stipulate deposit refunds in case of injury, sickness, or death. Some states even require this clause to be provided by licensed outfitters. Hunting consultants will often post hunts that have been cancelled for other reasons. Many times these hunts can be purchased, less the deposit, since it has already been paid. Keeping your ear to the ground can really pay off here.

Final payment for the hunt generally occurs at time of arrival or ten days prior to your arrival to allow time for a personal check to clear. The contract will be marked "paid" and you're on your way.

Believe me when I say that the entire process is relatively easy, and not as intimidating as it seems in print. Many hunters book a hunt right on the counter at a sport show.

Once the booking plans are taken care of travel arrangements to this far-flung part of the world are in order. Will you fly or drive? Early booking allows for more time to find airline ticket discounts. The airlines have printed information on the carrying of firearms, and trophy game heads and meat. Read these carefully. If you do decide to fly on a commercial airline, invest in a quality hard gun case. The case may take a good beating, but if it is a good one your rifle won't.

Sometimes hunters will be traveling as a party. In this case designate a captain or leader to take care of the arrangements. Whether booking or travel plans, one person can handle it with much less confusion.

Allow yourself time after the hunt. A full day of relaxing after the hunt can really help. The outfitter and butcher must combine forces to ready your animal for the trip home. It may be that the Game and Fish Department must check the animal. Occasionally shipping tags are needed in addition to the field tag. Go to town and buy the wife something. Enjoy the local flavor. Small towns in the heart of big game hunting always have a rich history.

For some reason it is finding and booking a hunt that stops many hunters right in their tracks. I guess it is the same with buying a new car. You want it. You may even feel you need it. It just seems like such a hassle to go out and do it. In reality, booking the hunt is simple enough. Other hunters do it everyday. Who knows, it might just be your turn.

*From your easy chair to places like this*

# Guide & Hunter
*Chapter III*

It was the last day of August. Even here in the mountains each passing day was one of heat and drought. John and I had set this wilderness sheep camp five days earlier, and I expected the outfitter and his sheep hunter to ride in at any time. Bighorn sheep season opened on September first and I had been scouting for a good ram for five days. My horses were picketed on grass and I fiddled around with my spotting scope outside my tent as they pulled in.

John led three pack mules and his hunter, Dan from Atlanta, Georgia, brought up the rear. Introductions completed, we unpacked the mules and turned them loose. Dan stowed his gear in his tent. His clothing looked fresh and crisp and he sported one of those new rifles with the composite stock and stainless barrel. He was of medium height and build, but I noticed that hawklike look of a hunter. You can't put your finger on it. It just is. Or isn't.

"Dan, Randy says he has a good one tied up already." John was always good for putting the pressure on his guides right off the bat.

I poured the iced tea and rolled out a topographic map on the kitchen table. I spotted 19 different rams and two of them were big ones. One was about three miles from camp living in a rocky gorge, a loner. I doubted seriously that we could even get to him due to the structure of the cliffs. The other was traveling with a younger ram on the mountain behind camp. These two held to the timber most of the day fighting the heat and flies. I only got two glimpses of them in five days.

I went over the lay of the land with John and Dan. A rarity in sheep hunting, two other camps were in the area. One camp had one sheep hunter and guide. The other camp had two resident hunters hunting together. That made four hunters in this range to bring in the opening day. The bulk of the rams I had spotted were within striking distance of the other two camps. The rams were nowhere close to the size of the one behind camp, and I felt none of the other hunters had gotten a look at him either.

Mutually it was decided over iced tea, that Dan and I would hunt on the mountain behind camp. John would tend camp and scout for rams with his spotting scope from our lookout on a knob just across from camp. Dan fired a few rounds down country to make sure his .300 was hitting the mark. I liked this hunter. He seemed at ease in his rifle handling abilities and well seasoned to camp life. Sheep hunters tend to evolve into the sport after hunting various types of other game. In our conversation, Dan informed me that he had bagged all western game with the exceptions of sheep and goat.

Evening was coming on and we figured we would have a look from our perch. We climbed the lookout knob with the ordinary huffs and puffs of high country hiking. I glassed across the main valley and I had Dan glassing behind camp for the two rams. Rams don't always stay in one place. In fact, they sometimes cover large tracts of country in their daily routines. The drought had left the country fairly dry but there was a seep just below timberline behind camp. Try as we might we didn't glass a single ram. Even some of the other sheep I knew about didn't show. We saw two ewes far off in the last gray of the evening.

At supper that night I had begun to second guess my plan. Perhaps I should head for the other rams. They were concentrated in familiar country, but though they were legal rams I knew where the big one was. John sensed my concerns, but left the decision to me. I had guided clients to rams several times in this country and he had faith in me. It's great working with people who have respect for each other's abilities.

We left camp at first light, such as it was anyway. Fog had rolled in during the night, thick enough to hand your coat on. We took our two saddle horses and pack mule as far as we could ride. Donning our pack frames, Dan and I climbed higher into the fog. We followed game trails at first in the timber. We broke out into boulders and stunted pines just shy of 9,000 feet. Nearly exhausted we rested on a talus slope around eight or nine in the morning. We couldn't see 75 yards in any direction. I knew it might take a couple of hours for the sun to burn it off.

At eleven a breeze blew the fog out and we had good visibility throughout the day. Try as I might, I could not find the two rams. We glassed the seep until it was almost dark, then headed down for the horses. I could see Dan felt a little disappointment but he never mentioned it.

We hunted around the corner of the mountain the second day. We assumed the rams were hanging out there as we could not get a view of it the day before. The second day was much like the first. We saw a few elk and even a beautiful silvertip grizzly, but no rams. That day John ran into one of the other hunters on the main trail. He had scored on a smallish ram on the fist day. His buddy was going to stay for his ram. The lucky hunter seemed happy enough mentioning that he only had a four-day vacation to hunt. John had only spotted a few ewes and no rams from the lookout.

We were coming up on Dan's third day and my eighth. He hadn't seen a ram yet. I was worried that he was worried. I knew full well that sheep hunting often goes like this. Dan took it all in stride. He said he was there to hunt. We would keep after our original plan one more day.

Day three dawned warm and still. The drought continued. We altered the plans a bit by climbing the mountain across from the little valley behind camp. This would give us a view of two sides of the mountain we wanted to hunt. I manned the spotting scope as Dan watched through his 10-power binoculars. As the morning passed we chatted about sheep, Dan's family, and how to ride bucking horses. We ate our snack lunches early out of boredom. We were pretty much wrapping up our life history to each other when I spotted them. A patch of white rump materialized, then another. Two rams were feeding under a formidable cliff. They were facing away from us as we watched from a mile and a half across the valley. Dan and I had glassed their location all morning to no avail, when they were simply....just there.

It was indeed the two rams we were hunting. The big one looked like he may go 180, but I didn't want to overestimate his size.

"I think he'll go 170. His buddy is no slouch either, Dan. He is somewhere around 160, I guess."

"Man he's big! Look how he's broomed off at the end. The curl drops way beneath his jaw too." Dan was excited. Me too for that matter.

We had been hunting hard, not unusual for sheep hunting, but this was like seeing a pot of gold at the end of the proverbial rainbow. This truly was an outstanding bighorn sheep. I piled rocks around my spotting scope for a dead rest. The rams turned and were feeding slowly down the mountain toward the same seep we had counted on right along.

"Here, take a look through the scope. I got it on thirty-power." Dan crawled in behind the scope. Squinting through the eye piece, he knew what he was looking at. He remained calm enough though. His prior hunting experience was showing now.

"Really Randy, how big is he? I know he's big enough, but what would you say?"

"I don't know. I guess him at 15 1/2 inch bases. Maybe 34 inch length. He's broomed off big at the end and he carries the mass well into the horn. He's probably better than 170. The other ram will go 160, and I'm going by that too."

"Well he's plenty big enough for me. What do we do?"

Dan was a little strained by then. It was nerves. I didn't blame him. I didn't want to blow this chance. We had to make a good stalk first. If we could get on him I felt Dan was hunter enough to get it done.

"We'll have to wait till they bed for the day. They should bed right near the seep. When they're down for good we'll plan our stalk to get above them. Hopefully we can hide behind those two pinnacles on the right. The wind should be right there too. We can stick to the timber to get most of the way, then go back around the contour before we move in.

" What had been so wrong for the two days before was now falling into place like clock work. Both rams bedded after a cool drink at the seep. The big one bedded twenty yards above the smaller ram. They blended in perfectly with the surrounding rocks. If we had started scoping at this point we might not have seen them at all. Football players must give each other the same look as they leave the huddle for the next play. Dan and I stared at each other briefly before we headed down the mountain.

We hit bottom at the creek. I refilled the canteens, knowing full well the climb ahead of us would be a long and grueling one. We stopped at the horses to drop off our extra clothes. The day was heating up and already sweat was forming under my shirt. I joked that this was really desert bighorn hunting. Dan was too preoccupied going through is pockets rechecking to make sure he had everything to even catch the lame joke. This was it and he had that grim look of determination. His occasional grin was only a forced response to mine.

It was 50 yard intervals at first. Three quarters of the way up we were stopping to rest every 25 yards. At times we used our hands to crawl up and over the rock outcroppings. We went over the variables at each stop.

I assured Dan the rams would stay. I was a bit worried about them leaving as well, but I kept from letting it show. There were no other hunters in the area. The wind was right. It was going on two o'clock and we had plenty of daylight. I hadn't seen any fresh grizzly sign. What could go wrong? We both were aware that this was hunting. Were we kidding each other?

An hour later we lay behind two pinnacles of rock that overlooked where the rams had bedded. The rubble at the base of the pinnacles made a saddle between them. It was steeper than I thought earlier. To get a look, Dan laid on his belly against the rubble. He put his outstretched arms up to make footholds with his hands. I crawled up and placed each boot in his palms to peek over the edge. I nearly gasped when I saw both rams in their original beds only 60 yards away. I lowered my head back down from the ridgeline and whispered for Dan to let me down. A few pebbles rolled down with my descent, and I fretted the rams might hear it.

"Okay, they're dead ahead at 60 yards." I whispered with a cupped hand right into Dan's ear. "The big one is on the right quartering away facing left."

Dan put a round in the chamber of his .300. He couldn't answer. He barely nodded his head. He was mentally off into the hunter's world of "the moment of truth." I assumed Dan's previous position and he scurried into the saddle. I held his feet for what was an eternity. My arms ached when the shot rang out. I held as steady as I could, waiting for the next round.

I couldn't see a thing and it was getting to me when Dan opened the bolt. The empty rolled on past me and I wondered why he didn't jam the next one home. Finally he yelled.

"I got him!"

I wasn't able to hold him up any longer. I lowered my arms and Dan and I slid into a pile at the base of the pinnacles. Without a word we gathered our pack frames and scrambled around the down hill side of the pinnacles. I grabbed Dan's pack rounding the corner. If he needed a second shot after all, I wanted him to be ready. We slid and fell several times in our excitement.

The smaller ram reluctantly vanished into the next ravine. Our prize lay exactly where he had bedded for the day. Dan rushed ahead rolling loose rocks down on me in his haste. This was is trophy ram. We had jumped through all the hoops and had hunted hard to get this far. I wanted Dan to be the first to lay human hands on this magnificent animal.

Dan and I took turns snapping photos of each other with the ram. Giddy with success we drank from our canteens and slapped each other on the back, reliving the hunt.

"I just can't believe it. At last...my ram." Dan went on and on.

I wanted to remain stoic, but his glee was contagious. We laid on our backs gazing up at the cloudless blue sky. There was work to be done, but for now at least, we simply wanted to appreciate the day. The hunt.

The ram scored 179 points according to my tape at the scene. Later the official score would tally 177 and five-eighths. He had 16 1/2 bases. The right horn was 34 plus, and the left horn was 36 inches long. He was broomed off on the tips with nearly a three-inch diameter at the end of the horn. He had thickness, or good mass, throughout the length.

I skinned the ram for a life-size mount. We boned the meat stuffing it into pillow cases I carried to keep the bundles clean. Dan shouldered the head and cape and his rifle. I burdened under a load of meat, camera equipment, and other gear. We started our descent at the same time the sun passed out of sight and the evening air cooled.

My bad knee ached as I held the weight back on each tentative step down the mountain. Dan twisted his ankle and fell skinning one knee and both of his hands. The moon was coming up by the time we got the mule packed and ready for the trip down to camp.

We rode along in the shadows the timber created beneath the moon. The animals were plenty anxious to get back having been tied to trees for 13 hours. I knew John would be concerned, but I figured there was a good chance he had heard the shot. We pulled into camp sore and tired.

Dan commented, "Are we having fun yet?"

John had a groove worn in the ground from pacing back and forth, but he did two back flips when he grabbed the mule and got a good look at the horns.

"Holy Cow! When I heard the shot I thought you might be just practicing," he was joking.

We packed up the next morning. John allowed Dan to lead the pack mule with the skull mounted on top of the load. The Georgian hunter had five days worth of beard and had lost several pounds, but he sat tall in the saddle all the way out.

Such is the case with guides and hunters. It takes team work. By putting two heads together and two sets of eyeballs scanning the slopes, the team is able to draw from each other's strengths. The outfitter puts it all together, the guide gets the hunter in position, and the hunter makes it work.

Guides come from all walks of life. They cover all age groups too, from 17 to 70. What a young guide lacks in experience, he makes up for in strength and exuberance. The old timer may not cover as much ground, but years of experience says he probably won't have to.

A guide must be able to get along with people. This quality means much more than you might think, since there may not be anyone else to talk to for days on end. Actually, it helps to be part psychologist to keep the hunter's spirits up through it all. The guide must be part zoologist and botanist in addition to being cook, doctor, woodsman, weatherman, taxidermist, legal advisor, ballistics expert, historian, geologist, tracker, mule packer, horse backer, hunter, veterinarian, whiskey drinker, and mechanic.

The hours on the job are generally 25 hours a day. It is almost always unbearably hot or numbing cold in the work place, and the guide is never permitted to go home. His work clothes and pajamas are the same. Wore out boots are the standard footwear required. Two right-hand gloves of different colors identifies the guide from everyone else in camp except the wrangler who has no gloves.

On the job the guides common mode of transportation may vary from region to region. Typically a guide must be able to handle a horse, pickup truck, snowmobile, four-wheeler, outboard motor boat, canoe, or airplane. In short, he must qualify to navigate anything other than the Nina, Pinta, and Santa Maria.

In the off season some guides find employment as rodeo cowboys, professional pool hustler, and international playboys. Mostly however, guides own a small business or work for hourly wages to gain a grub stake in hopes of purchasing their own outfitting business. Outfitters too, have their own delusions of grandeur, usually involving the control of entire continents.

Living in the woods most of the while doesn't necessarily leave the guide lacking should he be caught out of his element. Most guides with a few seasons under their belts have guided many influential people. Drop a guide smack into the metro section of Big Town, USA, and you will quickly find that one phone call can result in a limo rescue from a sea of humanity. The guide, a survivalist at all times.

Seriously, your guide will, more often than not, turn out to be quite professional at performing his work. Just like you, guides love to hunt. Actually, guides live to hunt. This in itself is enough to forsake more comfortable working conditions to be found almost anywhere else. I have known guides from all part of the world, and with many types of backgrounds, yet this need to hunt runs as true in good guides as it does in good hunting dogs.

The hunter often feels a kind of subliminal pressure to be successful on his guided hunt. Some of this is simple enough, as a hunter want to get game. More of it tends to be obscured. Friends at home may be envious of your opportunity to go on some exotic excursion to far off places. These peers may even chide you about it. Family budgets are often tight so that a hunting trip may only be possible once in a blue moon. Getting the game may justify the cost, but it shouldn't be the only reason we hunt. The guide feels this pressure too. He realizes that his hunter has a substantial time and expense investment in the hunt. The outfitter uses today's success to promote next year's business. Some guides may equate hunting success with their tips, though I have not found this to be the case.

Guide and hunter should be there to hunt to the best of their ability. It is a time to have some fun and hone outdoor skills. The guided hunt is a positive experience. Time and money must be left at the airport. Hunting the trophy animal is paramount to anything else.

It is amazing how long friendships last between guide and hunter. I've been at this game a good long time and I still get cards or phone calls from hunters I may never see again. Living the hard life, or good life, for a week or more creates a bond of trust. The trust comes from mutual respect.

Mike and I were flat on our bellies glassing the semiarid desert that sprawled below our lookout. The sun had already dipped well below the horizon and the gray light of twilight seemed contradicted by the bright orange streaks across the western sky. The antelope were mere dots on the plains, but I was zeroing in on the buck with my scope. Prickly pear cactus jabbed at us. Mike commented on the cool breeze of the evening.

We were putting a good antelope buck to bed. Antelope don't travel much at night and we figured to be on him the next morning. We had already spent two days on this buck, however, he and his does kept to a large flat expanse that would not allow us a stalk. There was a better than even chance that this buck would book. Mike had already taken two record book antelope during his hunting career, but he had a passion for antelope hunting, explaining to me that he had hunted them for more than 30 years.

Mike was 32 years my senior. A self-made millionaire, he had hunted all over the world, His age and years of experience gave him a quiet patience that really set me at ease to guide him in any way I saw fit. In the fading light we sipped the last drops from our canteens.

"Mike, I think we can crawl up on him from the south in the dark tomorrow morning. The wind should be right, but it will be at least a mile of hunkering down even in the dark. I don't know where they're getting their water, but they ain't leaving that flat."

"Yea, your right, but these old bones might not make it that far. Besides, all this cactus will leave us looking like a couple of pin cushions. Let's think about it some more on the way back to town.

" We picked our way off the butte in the dark. Mike walked tentatively 50 yards behind, and I would wait for him. He had given up elk hunting and sheep hunting some years earlier. He was well acquainted with the rigors of the mountain. He loved to hunt though, and we weaved our way across the flat dark prairie toward the pickup. A lone coyote howled a mournful tune at the night sky.

I threw my pack frame in the bed of the truck and Mike pointed out the Big Dipper. Down the dusty two tracks we went, jack rabbits running from the headlights. We traded the mournful tune of the coyote for the mournful tunes of country music on the radio. Empty soda cans rolled around our feet each time I hit a rut in the road the wrong way.

"Ya know, you really have it made Randy."

"Well, I don't know about that. I..."

"No, you do. You make a living doing what you enjoy, and that is really what it's all about. Trust me, it is."

I could barely make out the lights from town through the dirty windshield. Thinking about what he said I couldn't get over it. Here he was a millionaire. He flew in on his own plane, he had hunted three different continents. And I had it made? Bills to pay? A wore out pickup?

Mike was all right. He trusted my judgement. He had actually hunted antelope longer than I had, yet he knew I knew. I liked that, and as a result I hunted harder than I might have otherwise. The gray haired guy bouncing on the seat next to me wasn't a client. He was my hunting buddy.

We ate a late dinner at the local cafe. Mike entertained me with tales of cape buffalo and hippos. The waitress finally grew impatient and threw us out so she could close up. Walking across the parking lot I started going over the plan for the morning. Mike nodded in agreement as we walked.

"Yep, that'll work all right. It's a good plan, but I think I'll pull out first thing tomorrow."

I stopped dead in my tracks. Slack-jawed. I couldn't believe what he had just said. He was leaving now? Just when we had this buck nailed down?

"Don't look so hang dog. You've done a great job showing me a book buck. That sky tonight meant weather is coming tomorrow and I can fly out before it gets here if I get up early. Besides, I can't crawl that far. We both know that."

"Okay, I know of some other bucks. We can try to get on them instead." I still couldn't believe he would leave early without an antelope.

"Look, it ain't the killin.' It's the huntin.' I know you've got a job to do, but you've done it. And, you did it right. I'm satisfied. I had a good hunt. It doesn't have to be a long hunt to be a good hunt. I don't have to kill to have it be a good hunt. I used to, but time changes things sometimes. Ya know."

Not saying much, I dropped Mike off at his motel room. I was too inexperienced to understand. It was funny. Mike felt bad for me, and didn't give a wit about getting "his" antelope. I'll never forget what he said.

"You got it wrong, Randy. It's not "my" antelope. It's God's antelope until I shoot it. If I choose not to shoot, I'm not leaving something that's mine, now am I?"

I thought about it, and Mike saw the concern on my face. He turned it into a joke.

"Look at it this way. What if I shot at my antelope and missed and hit "your" antelope by mistake?"

Mike was quite a guy. I'll never forget what he said. In fact, with each passing year I understand a little more and a little more.

Guides and hunters. Somewhere in the world a guide and his hunter are hunting this very minute. Together they are seeking game, going over all the variables that must be taken into account. Sometimes serious, sometimes comic, the hunt bonds them. If they work as a team, as would a pair of coyotes, the whole endeavor will most likely pan out. If they do not, it will not.

Guides ply their trade generally after some training. Yes, actual hunting may certainly be the best training, but it is much easier to get yourself on game than it is to get yourself and your hunter on game. Two or three people make that much more noise and leave that much more scent than a lone hunter.

Guides may start as wranglers, packers, or cooks and wood cutters. Today, guide schools are available to those who want to learn as well. These "guide" schools teach, but one must have the basic desire and outdoor experience to graduate and expect to land a job.

First aid training is important, especially so when most of the work is done in the back country. This is a poor place for carelessness with an axe or the like. Many states require certification in first aid to maintain a guides license. In a different note, but along the same vein, I get mighty anxious when a hunter waits until we are on the mountain to reveal his bad heart condition. Sometimes they tell the guide that they didn't want to cause the outfitter any concern, so they didn't bring it up when they booked the hunt. This doesn't do much as far as getting the guide to tear up the mountain side looking for game.

Your guide should be familiar with the country he's guiding in. I have done well in unfamiliar country, but I had a thorough knowledge of the species I was after. To be in position before daylight, and getting back after dark though still puts knowledge of the lay of the land at the top of the list.

Guides must be able to handle an animal after it is downed. Proper care of meat and trophy is, after all, part of what the client is paying for. An experienced guide has the tools necessary for this task on hand always.

It seems as though every state and province has far different game laws. Your guide must have a complete understanding of these regulations, and keep current on changes from year to year. The guide may have to advise you on the rules in a heartbeat. Take the advise. It is always a good idea to read the rules long before the hunt takes place as well.

You may find yourself hunting with a different guide each day in some camps. This is not common, but it happens. I believe that a guide and hunter need some time to get used to each other and recommend you stick with the same guide for the duration of the hunt. If your guide hunts too fast or too slow, work it out together. If you learn each other's habits early on it is unquestionably better to do so now than to go through a new process every day with a new partner. Of course, if it is a hopeless case of oil and water, you may talk with the outfitter about a different guide. Remember though that there are not any extra guides standing around camp, so you may have to trade guides with another hunter. Not always easy.

By and large I would have to say that today's guides are more professional than they used to be. Sure, this is a generalization, but the competitiveness of the business today demands better service.

*Guide and Hunter,*

*... The Team that makes it work.*

# Shoot, Shoot, Shoot
## Chapter IV

The last hunter went off toward his tent, disappearing into the darkness. Harvey threw a couple of good logs on the campfire and pulled up another to sit on.

"Hey buckaroo. Come on over and have a pull 'for ya turn in."

Harvey really enjoyed a good pull on the bottle of Jim Beam before bed. I figured I'd sit down for one myself at his invitation. After all, one of my hunters had killed a good bull that day, and I owed it to myself to celebrate a little.

It went down smooth, burning a bit when it hit bottom. The glow from the fire and firewater were hitting me at the same time, inside and out. It felt kind of good. My body ached from hoisting the meat up into the meat pole. This bit of relaxation was a welcome one. Besides, Harvey was always good for a grizzly bear story or some bit of mountain philosophy.

He had guided hunters in this part of the country during his entire adult life. At 60-years-old, Harvey was still plenty fit owing it to "clean livin" as he put it. He was a colorful character to be sure, but he was an honest man and never did I underestimate his abilities. Harvey was a little slower at packing his loads, but his packs never slipped once he pointed his mules down the trail. Any trail.

Harvey tilted his old gray cowboy hat back on his head. He was getting ready and I recognized the gesture.

"Well, this is my last season. I'm sellin the mules and keepin' to town from here on out." He punctuated this statement with another pull of JB.

"Whad a ya mean? It looks like ya got a couple of seasons left in ya Harvey. Things won't be the same without ya. You ain't that old. What are we supposed to do, name a crick after ya?"

"Well them guys can't hit nothin no more. They barely know which end to point, and I'm tired of working all day just to miss some bull or maybe not even get the shot off in the first place."

"Harvey, guys miss sometimes, you know that. Hell, I miss sometimes too. If ya shoot your gonna miss sometimes." I was trying to cheer him up.

"I know, I know, but it's gettin worse. Can't you see it?"

I stared into the fire and thought about it. I hadn't guided as long as old Harvey, but maybe he had a point. I had witnessed more blown shots than I really cared to remember. It might not have been of epidemic proportions, but it was something to think about. Hunters get excited. That's why we hunt. It's exciting. Some hunters have trouble judging distances. That's nothing new. Even so, these hunters did seem to have trouble getting the shot off and hitting what they were shooting at.

I went off to my own tent thinking about it some more. I have been thinking about this shooting thing for some time now and here are my thoughts.

I don't think today's hunter spends enough time with his rifle. Bow hunters tend to practice for hours on end. Rifle hunters on the other hand think that these modern rifles are so keen that little or no practice is necessary. Some hunters even look awkward handling their gun. As harsh as this criticism might seem, let me elaborate.

I think it's easy to go out and shoot up a bunch of shotgun shells. Liberal bird seasons allow for much practice. Then too, the shotgun is a short range weapon and because of that safe shooting is easy to come by. Shooting a bunch of sporting clays can be real fun for a group of buddies on Sunday afternoon.

By contrast it is not as easy for some to find a place to practice with a center fire high powered rifle. Practicing with your rifle may require a long drive to the rifle range or countryside. Deer season, because of shorter time periods and fewer bag limits, doesn't give some folks much of a chance either. Even if one has a good place to practice, many find it much more pleasurable to explode sporting clays than it is to walk out and check the bull's-eye 200-300 yards down range.

Nevertheless, we owe it to ourselves and the game we hunt to be proficient with the rifles we use. Practice here does not require the hours of dedication that bow hunters put in, but practice comes in many forms.

There is no good substitute for actual shooting at various distances. A hunter should be expected to be accurate at 300 yards with most modern rifle calibers and a good rifle scope. Of course, this requires shooting from a bench rest at first. I usually advise hunters to sight their rifles to be dead on at 200 yards You may be slightly low at 300 in this case or slightly high at 100 yards Still you will be right in there with say a six-inch bull from 100-300 yards if the rifle is shot on at 200.

Most folks are content to shoot at 100 yard targets or less, figuring that they can calculate bullet drop at various ranges when the time comes. Wrong. In an actual hunting situation, there are far too many other things to think about. Is the animal moving? Is the wind blowing? Do I have a clear line of sight? At the moment of truth there are things to do besides the things to think about. You may have to quickly get a round into the chamber. You might have to remove the scope covers. You should be going for a rest, whether it be a solid rest, three-point position, or a prone position. Maybe you'll only have time to use your rifle sling as a wrap around rest. There are plenty of good reasons not to burden yourself with last second mathematics.

Shooting your rifle at 200 yard targets accomplishes something else too. You will get used to looking at things farther away and hitting them. This builds confidence. Confidence is the single greatest gift to shooting well. I have personally observed hesitation piled on top of hesitation while the animal walked off without a shot being fired. It is far better to shoot and miss than to not shoot at all, but confidence remedies both most of the time.

I do most of my hunting with my little 30-30 Winchester. It's a model 94 lever action with iron sights. I have a fancy seven mag. That has dropped many animals in their tracks, but my little saddle gun gives me pleasure. It reminds me of being a kid again. I took my first deer with a 30-30. To be accurate with it I have to stalk in close and I enjoy a sneaky sneak. I like 100 yard shots or less, but I practice at 200 yards. My front sight covers up quite a bit at that range, but I'm still good at two if I have to be. Practice.

On rainy days or evenings you can practice gun handling in the basement or the garage. You don't need a loaded gun because you're not actually shooting.. Just practice pulling the gun into your shoulder and sighting on the target. Repetition pays off. Work the lever or bolt without taking the rifle down from the shooting position. Keeping the target in the sight picture aids greatly in a second or even third shot situation. If you want to practice trigger pull, place an empty cartridge in the chamber to give the firing pin something to land on. Please make sure you're using an empty cartridge. It won't do any good to load up the magazine with empties as they won't feed well.

I have pictures of deer and bears and what not on the wall. These animals are in all different poses and it gives me wonderful practice to pull up on these as opposed to a dry old black bull's-eye. This soon has the cross hairs or sights landing right on the animal's vital area. Again, try to work the action while holding on the target. All of this can be done without going to the rifle range.

It is best to obtain a rest while shooting at game. Sometimes you may be forced to shoot off hand but if you're using your head you can quickly get a rest without wasting too much time. I think it goes without saying that a rock or log is good, but it might be several feet away and you could blow your cover if you try to get to it, thus spooking the game.

A three point position works well. One point is your butt. The other two points are each one of your feet. Just sit down on the ground planting each foot solidly. Wrap your arm into the rifle sling for extra rigidity. When you pull the rifle up, leave each elbow planted down solidly on each knee. If you haven't tried this you'll be amazed how steady it is and how easy it is to work the action from this position.

A prone position is simply one of lying flat on your belly, slightly cocked off to the side of the direction you intend to shoot. Dig both elbows into the ground and make sure the rifle is firmly pushed back into your shoulder. It will be a little more difficult to work the bolt from a prone position. Sometimes too, the eye relief of your scope seems to change. Given this it is still better than an off hand shot.

Shooting sticks work well as a rifle rest. These are two sticks about four foot long tied together with twine at 15 inches from one end. The two sticks work as a pair of scissors with the twine acting as the hinge. Spread the sticks and place each one into the ground with the short end of the scissors upward to lay your rifle in. Sit down and adjust the sticks to the right height by spreading the legs, or bringing them closer together. The forearm part of the rifle stock should lay in the top "V" or the "X." Never lay the barrel in the groove. This will result in poor accuracy. If you're a right handed shooter use your left hand to hold the forearm solidly, pressing down into the "V."

There are a few companies manufacturing shooting sticks and mono sticks from metal or plastics. I find that two sticks picked up in the field work well. When we leave the area I just untie them and pocket the twine to move on. We have enough equipment to carry, and I can always get new sticks at the next spot, unless, of course, we find ourselves in very open country.

Occasionally when sitting on a stand or blind we set the sticks up well before any game shows up. Place the rifle in the sticks pointed in the direction you expect to see game. Pull the rifle back slightly and rest the butt of the stock on the ground. This makes a tripod with one leg being your rifle. Now you can free up your hands for other things while you wait. Very little movement is needed to get ready for the shot, a big plus.

Young George had built his own rifle. At 20 years of age, this feat impressed me, needless to say, and I admired his .264 Win Mag. It was a stainless version with a beautiful stock, rosewood I think. I had guided George's father to several good mule deer and at his father's request I was now guiding the next generation of fine shooters this family had to offer.

George wanted a long shot. He thought much more of a good long shot than he did of the size of the buck he was after. His father had made one shot kills with me before and I guessed this kid had probably been trained well. He handled his rifle well, worked the loads up himself and was confident out to 400 yards

I asked him about wind drift with a lighter caliber and bullet penetration should his hot loads be moving too fast. He had all the bases covered. His straight six power scope had fine cross hairs, and I noticed he only put one shell in the chamber at the deer stand. He figured the gun heated up too much with these loads to allow for any more accurate shots after the first one.

Our time came when a decent buck appeared with three does, all traveling the migration trail to their wintering grounds. The buck was a three point by western standards and I knew we could do better. The buck would pass our stand at about 400 yards to our left.

"Let's wait George. I know a bigger one will come by sooner or later."

"I want him. There's no wind and he's moving along real slow."

"Okay, when he gets to that opening I'll coyote howl at him to stop him. You have to be ready at that point."

The buck brought up the rear sniffing the ground behind the does. The rut would start in a week and he was catching the doe scent, intoxicated by it. I really wanted to send this kid home with a good four point. His father would expect it. But it was George's call. He liked the looks of the buck and loved the setup of this shot.

The deer were traveling sideways across the opposite mountain side. We were set up on a hill across a medium sized valley, but at the same elevation with the deer. George was sitting behind a large lava rock half laying across the top of it peering through his scope. The deer were far from us and failed to notice as he scooted around to get the most comfortable position. We were poised and ready. It was the time all guides and hunters work so hard for, and dream of until it happens.

"Are you ready George?"

"Yea."

"Okay, I guess it at four. Hold a little high..."

He cut me off. "It's 375. I know where to hold."

I was mildly shocked. I was used to explaining distances, sometimes repeatedly to hunters. I couldn't help but marvel at his coolness at his age. He had never taken a mule deer buck. This was his first guided hunt to boot.

"Okay, here goes."

The buck hit the clearing as the does were almost through it. I howled a long coyote howl at the deer. I was surprised when he kept walking as if nothing had happened. I was ready to howl again when the buck stopped to look our way. The distance it took for the sound to get to the deer caused the delay.

That howl was the last thing that buck ever heard. He dropped like a rock, and I honestly can't tell till this day which came first, the dropping deer or the bang of the gun. Coolly the kid ejected his spent round and put it in his pocket. He left the bolt open and turned to me grinning.

"God, I knew this gun could do it!"

"You did it George. You did it."

That same year I was guiding another deer hunter to what turned out to be "the miracle deer."

Ralph had a slide action .270 Remington. He had a four power rifle scope of poor quality and three different brands of ammo all rolling around together in his coat pocket. You guessed it. I started getting that sinking feeling even before we got going.

Ralph wanted to get a deer. He informed me that he would take any legal buck. He just didn't want to go home empty handed. We waited along a good trail in the bitter cold of predawn. He had lost one of his gloves the day before and his hooded sweatshirt did little to keep him warm. The poor guy shivered uncontrollably, and I considered building a small fire for humanitarian purposes.

The sun was barely coming over the mountain when the first buck of the day came wandering down the trail He was about 400 yards out, headed our way, when I pointed him out to Ralph.

"Here comes a small one. He's moving nice and easy. If you want him, get ready."

"Yea..a..a I I I wwant him." The poor guy shivered even worse at the sight of the buck.

"Okay, lay your rifle over this rock."

"He's too oo oo ffar away, aint' he?"

"Yea, but this will give you a chance to get set before he is in range. Go ahead."

Ralph laid his gun down on the hard rock. I quickly slipped my hat under the rifle. Ralph tried to stand and bend over at the waist to look into the scope. I placed a hand on his shoulder to induce him into taking a kneeling position behind the rock.

"Okay, Ralph, you got him in the scope?"

"No, I can't see nothin. Oh, I see him. Should I shoot?'

"Not yet. He's still out a range. Go ahead and put a round in the chamber."

Ralph tried to slide the action open and proceeded to grind off the finish on the forearm against the abrasive rock.

"Lift the gun up Ralph."

When opened the action a live round plopped into the snow and he jammed a new one home. He had a live round in there and neither one of us knew it. I knelt down to find the one in the snow and worked well behind the hunter. I had been off to his left, but now I was looking for cover with one eye while keeping the other on the deer. I tried to coach the nervous hunter as the buck came on. I noticed that he held his left hand on top of the scope, I guessed it was his way of steadying it. The deer was close enough now that I didn't dare try to correct much more.

"Okay, he's 100...." Boom.

The gun went off before I could get the words out. The deer went down hard, and Ralph jumped up. In his excitement he nearly fell from the little shelf we were standing on and his clip fell out and rolled a couple of feet down the incline.

"Gimme the shells out of your pocket Ralph!"

The deer looked as if he had a broken spine and though he tried to get up he floundered helplessly in the snow. Ralph got some shells to me and dropped more in the snow.

"Now put a round in the chamber and finish him off."

"I gotta have the clip to do that."

"You don't need the clip. Just open the receiver and hand feed a round in."

"I never done that before."

I got hold of the rifle and hand fed a round in. Ralph was grabbing at the rifle and I had to turn my back on him to get the job done. Facing the deer I handed the loaded weapon back to him with the muzzle pointed toward the sky.

"Now calm down Ralph, He ain't goin nowhere, but we gotta finish him off. Take your time."

Ralph fired five rounds at the same deer, he hit on the first shot and missed every time. I was beside myself. I loaded each consecutive round for him and he went right on missing. The remaining ammo lay in the snow at various points.

The deer seemed to be regaining his previously healthy condition and even looked as if he might get up at any second. I had a revolver with me but I doubted it's accuracy at this range. Guides are not permitted to finish off game for their hunters in Wyoming. A game law violation could easily result in the loss of one's guides license too. I thought about running over to the deer, but I was afraid to leave Ralph with the rifle.

"Gimme that rifle Ralph."

I found a shell in the snow and loaded the rifle and took aim. The cross hairs were completely out of whack. The scope was actually wallowing around inside the scope rings. Later Ralph told me that was why he was holding down on the top of the scope before the first shot was fired. I couldn't believe this state of affairs.

I grabbed my hat and two more rounds I thumbed out of the faulty clip.

"Come on Ralph, we gotta run over there and shoot him point blank."

We started for the deer. I had the rifle, my .45, and an unarmed hunter. The deer has been hit under the spine, shocking it considerably but not breaking the spine or damaging any vital organs. The buck jumped up before we went ten yards.

"There he goes Randy! Do something!"

I shouldered that rifle and pointed it like shotgun. With one pull of the trigger I downed the buck and broke the law at the same time. I can't begin to explain all that I felt at that moment. A great shot. The deer was no longer suffering. Did this mean I was a hopeless outlaw? I wondered if any guide ever gutted his hunter.

Ralph hollered in exuberance. "You got him!"

"Shut up Ralph."

Ralph danced around the deer as I worked to tag it for him and get it ready for the drag down the mountain. Later the game warden listened to my pathetic story and let me off the hook. He kept looking at Ralph as I explained, nodding his head at my words, and shaking his head at the sight of Ralph fumbling with his rifle. Ralph appeared oblivious to the gravity of the entire situation. He had is deer.

It is suffice to say that this scenario isn't typical. Most hunters handle their firearms well, and are familiar with the operating of the same. I asked Ralph why he hadn't handled his rifle more. He said he had always kept it well hidden in the attic since his wife would probably hock it if she ever found out he had it.

The entire hunt centers on the "shot." Airplane tickets, hunt costs, clothing, vacation, and all the rest comes together at the shot. I am always amazed when a hunter is reluctant to fire his gun before the hunt. That same hunter seems to always set his rifle down against a tree and sort of walk off 10 feet away from it. It's as if he doesn't like this rifle, and cares not to spend any time with it.

I am also leery of the pretty gun. You know, the one with all the finest detail work and not a scratch on it. I have had some hunters say, "This is the nicest rifle I've ever owned, but I left my regular gun at home." At this point a guide finds himself longing for the "regular" rifle he has never seen. Three-thousand dollar rifles worry me. Like fine china, they don't get much use, thus hunter/rifle performance can be less than expected.

What rifle caliber is best? This argument will never be settled. I won't attempt to go through all the different calibers and loads for each. There is plenty of stuff out there if you want to study.

I want a flat shooting rifle that can knock an animal off it's feet. I want a rifle that is light enough to carry all day and require little cleaning. A bolt action is my first choice while a lever action is my second. Today's stainless models with composite stocks are a great choice.

Other than the actual shooting practice required to bag the game there are some tips that can help alleviate a long trial and error process to successful hunting. Bipods mounted on rifles are an excellent rest for shooting but the bulk of the bipod doesn't allow the rifle to be transported in a leather rifle scabbard on the saddle or hard scabbard commonly used on four wheelers and snowmobiles.

The same can be said for extra wide rifle slings. These slings are comfortable when slung over the shoulder, although they seldom fit into the scabbard while attached to the rifle.

Oil, gun grease, and even spray on silicone can impede the workings of your rifle in cold weather. In addition these lubricants also collect dirt and dust, sometimes causing the receiver to work hard or even jam. I recommend a clean, dry action. Protective oil on the outside of the rifle may be all right, but keep the working parts dry.

When working the action of any rifle, work it hard and deliberate. Mincing around with the action will result in the spent round failing to come out or prevent the new round from loading well into the chamber. This mechanical failure, due to soft handling, is termed as "short shucking."

Chamber a round only when your guide advises you to do so. You should not chamber a round while traversing difficult terrain or riding your horse, or all terrain vehicle. Never chamber a round in a vehicle.

Some hunters bring a backup rifle on the hunt. This is a good idea if you have one. For obvious reasons your second gun is ready if something unfortunate happens to your first rifle.

I like medium weight bullets for the caliber of gun I am using. Mid-sized bullets with a good powder load behind them get the most from the rifle. Heavy bullets drop quickly at long ranges, while light weight bullets tend to be drifted by the wind. Penetration and trajectory are best served with medium weight bullets.

Rifle scopes can be fitted with a wide array of scope covers. I've seen them all. Still, my favorite scope cover is the stretch type that stretches over the length of the scope covering both ends. This type of cover can be quickly removed as compared to spring loaded flaps or cup-type covers. A simple piece of inner tube works well.

Plan to arrive for your hunt to allow time to shoot. Don't take it for granted that the rifle made the trip in good shape until you fire it. If the outfitter hasn't made time for this in his busy schedule, take it upon yourself to do so. There is much going on at this point of arrival, but you and your rifle may well be the most important considerations. Don't fall into the trap of not having time to shoot.

Safe gun handling cannot be stressed enough. I could include some tragic stories, though I choose not to. If you haven't attended a hunter's safety course, by all means do so. The muzzle, trigger, and safety on that weapon should be as familiar to you as if they were a part of your own body. I have been fortunate enough in that I have not been in on any hunting accidents, but I have witnessed the results of accidents that took place. Let's keep this whole thing fun.

*Practice Pays off*

# The Horseback Hunt
*Chapter V*

The classic western hunt is the horseback hunt. In many parts of the U.S. and Canada, the Rocky Mountains lend themselves to this style of hunting. Roadless tracts of land holds game, and such was the case when I guided Tony on his spring black bear hunt.

It was mid-May and the slopes were a bright green with new grass running right up slope to the rapidly receding snow line. Herds of mule deer and elk grazed along at ease. Hunting seasons and a tough winter were a dim memory. Their blotchy coats were a mixture of new hair and bleached out old hair. The new grass was as delicious to the animals as it was lifesaving, their stores of fat gone and new birth yet to take place.

The bears too, relished this grass. Black bears and grizzly bears would graze like cattle on the open slopes. The nearby timber gave the black bear a quick haven in case of trouble. The snow fields cooled the grizzly during the heat of the day. Tony and I road our horses along and glassed the slopes. It felt good to be alive here in the sunshine in the heart of the Rockies. Thomas Jefferson once said, "The outside of a horse is good for the inside of a man."

Tony seemed to agree, grinning much of the time as he rode his mount, Timber.

"Man, this is like something out of Zane Grey. I can't get over it, riding along with my rifle here in my scabbard, seeing this, and living it." He beamed at the grandeur of it all.

"Hey, I see something up there on the top of that slide." I pointed and Tony squinted to see where I meant.

We tied up to two pines along the trail and I put the glasses on the bear. Tony jerked his rifle from the scabbard though the bear was a good half mile up the mountain.

"It's a grizz," I said as Tony came over to my vantage point.

"Boy, I wish we could hunt grizzlies. That's the fourth one we've seen on this hunt in three days." Tony talked as he watched the big silver bear through his scope.

The grizzly was grazing on new grass. We had spotted a fair-sized black black bear the day before, but he gave us the slip. I say black black bear because many western bears are cinnamon, chocolate, or even blonde. This grizzly though was feeding in a slide created by a winter avalanche of snow taking out all the trees and exposing that part of the mountain side to bare earth that had regenerated into grass. Black bears do the same thing this time of year. Spotting and stalking is a good way to hunt them.

"Well, I doubt any blacks are comin' around here since he has it staked out. Let's ride up the trail to the next slide and have a look."

Tony nodded and grabbed his horse. He was coming along real well. The first day I had to hold his horse for him and help him on. Now he was getting on and off, tying up and handling his rifle and scabbard on his own. He looked at this horseback stuff as a pleasant challenge. Tony had never been "a horseback" as we say, except as a kid at the occasional riding stable. He liked this buckaroo way of doing things and he asked a million questions. Tony was a quick learner.

I hid the horses in the timber at the base of the next slide about a mile up the trail from the previous bear sighting. Tony and I took a seat at the base of a big fir off to the side of the opening that stretched up the slope between the dark stands of timber. It is hard to use up all the daylight at this time of year. The daytime arrives at 5:30 or so, and night settles in at 8:30 in the evening. Bears can be active at any time but evenings are best. The shadows were getting long as the sun dipped below the mountain. I walked over to the horses to get our jackets from the backs of the saddles. I was untying my jacket when Tony whispered at the top of his lungs.

"Bear!"

I quickly got my hands on both jackets thinking we may need them should we have to leave the horses and stalk our way up the mountain. I sneaked back to our tree to see Tony peering intensely up the slide.

He pointed and whispered, "There he is. I think it's one of those chocolate black bears."

He was right. The bear was contentedly grazing near the top of the slide just underneath the snow. It was a long way up and I was afraid we might run out of daylight before we could get up there. This bear looked about average as size goes, but his coat was beautifully thick and shiny even in the shadow of the mountain. I figured it would take too much time to hike that far. If we tried it I was sure we would make too much noise in our haste.

Tony had a nervous grin on his face when he asked, "What do we do now?"

"I think we'll get on the horses and ride up that timbered draw off to the right. I've been in there before, and I think the horses can make it. They can get the elevation a lot quicker than we can, and the bear shouldn't hear us since we'll be down in the next draw. If we do it, we better go now though."

Tony slid his rifle into the scabbard and hurriedly put on his jacket while I untied the horses. We had to cross the open country at the bottom of the slide to get to the other side to start up the draw. If we could get across the bottom without spooking the feeding bear, I guessed that we had a pretty good chance.

We kept close together and walked the horses. I didn't want the bear to look down and see the animals moving fast. At a quiet walk, even if he spotted us, it might not cause alarm. We pulled into the trees and I peeked through the branches to see the brown bear still feeding peacefully some 600 yards up the slope.

"Okay Tony, this will be a little rougher than what we've done so far. Keep your horse close and right behind me. It's steep so you'll have to give him his head. Hang on to that saddle horn and lean forward. If you come close to a tree, just push off of it so you don't hit your knee or your rifle against the tree."

Tony nodded at the instructions. He was in the hunter's mode now, intense and sharp.

"Whatever you say, I just want to get a crack at him."

We started up the gut of the draw. Downed timber and large firs became a maze that we weaved our way through on faint game trials. It was getting fairly dark in the timber by this time, but our horses huffed their way higher and higher. We stopped halfway to let them blow. With a hand signal, I motioned to Tony to ride up close to me.

"You're doin' good cowboy. Now it's gettin' steep. We're goin' to switch back up the rest of the way. Make sure your horse does just what my horse does. Don't let him try to take a short cut on the switch back or he'll poop out on the steep hillside. If you have to get off, get off on the uphill side so you don't tip him over."

*The Horseback Hunt*

Tony was now getting all the Zane Grey he wanted. I had to give him credit. He was a game rooster. Usually you don't have to use your horses like this. I was gambling that Tony could handle it, and so far he was proving he could. He was well mounted too. I had named this horse "Timber" for this very reason. He was a good horse in timbered country. The roan gelding was sure-footed and levelheaded when the going got tough. He was a bit on the skinny side, though he possessed good wind and a strong heart, or what you might call a willingness to work.

The draw petered out near the top, providing us with less cover. As we rode the last yards the going became labored as the horses tired in the now rocky ravine. I felt my own horse getting weak in his hind legs and sweat lathered up on his neck. I found a level spot barely large enough to stand the two animals on and pulled up to let them rest.

"We gotta' stop here, Tony. The bear should be over the rise and slightly below us if he hasn't moved. There's nothing to tie to here. I'll have to hold these two while you crawl up and try to get a shot. Get off here and chamber a round. Make sure a grizz hasn't moved in and your shootin' at the bear we saw." I whispered almost out of breath, as if I had done the climbing.

Tony slipped from the saddle and jerked his rifle. He worked the action, checked the safety, and crouched low as he worked his way up the rise. I wished I'd had a place to tie up. If I turned the horses loose they may start for home without us, or top out on the rise spooking the bear. Tony was on his own.

My hunter disappeared over the rise and I stood holding the horses, yearning to hear the shot. It came once, then a pause, then twice more close together. I jumped on my horse and led Timber, headed for the top. Mentally I had my fingers crossed as I cleared the rise and looked into the slide.

At first I saw nothing. No Tony. No bear. Then I spotted Tony kneeling by a dark object down the slope. I spurred my way down to meet up with my ecstatic hunter. When he heard me coming up behind him, Tony turned to me and held his rifle above his head letting out a war whoop in true Comanche fashion.

Tony told the story as I hobbled the horses. We took our pictures with Tony's camera that he kept in the saddle bags. The flash of the camera startled our grazing horses, but they were hobbled and too tired to really care. He was a beautiful bear that lay before us. Tony's first bear.

He sat down on the damp ground next to his bear and shook his head. "I'll never forget this. Everything about this is just how I dreamed it would be."

"I'm glad, Tony. There is nothing like bear hunting, but right now you watch for grizzlies while I skin your bear." The reality check slowly brought the hunter back to earth.

I slung the hide across my saddle. My horses had been in on bear kills before and didn't mind the smell of bear. Some do however, and this doesn't work with all horses. I asked Tony if he wanted any meat. In Wyoming, a bear is classified as a trophy animal, as is a mountain lion. It is not mandatory to take out the meat as it is with all game animals. Tony decided he would like to try some, so I tied one haunch onto his saddle horn. Personally, I don't care much for bear meat, especially spring bears.

"Isn't it a waste to leave the rest?" Tony asked.

"The grizzlies will probably have it cleaned up by morning. They gotta' eat too. Besides, it's like leaving a coyote or coon. You can eat them, but can you really consider them food? I can pack it all out if you want. It's up to you."

"No, you're right. I don't s'pose those guys up north pack out and eat those grizzlies they get."

"Yea, and I haven't heard of anyone eating African lions or leopards either. There's nothing wrong with trophy hunting. This bear will make a fine rug. The '90s has everybody second guessing each other. Elk and deer are one thing. Bears and mountain lions are something else. These so called new attitudes are dreamed up by people who haven't done anything themselves anyway." I blurted out my views, but I believed it then and I believe it now.

Here we were, two hunters under the night sky. We led our mounts down the slide to the trail below. The stars twinkled bright and Tony let out a big sigh when he hit the saddle.

"What a night. I've never seen anything so beautiful. Even in the dark you can see the snow on the peaks."

"You know Tony, Teddy Roosevelt hunted this same valley."

"Man, they'll never believe it back home. Here we are riding our horses around in the dark with a bear across the saddle."

A coyote howled interrupting Tony, and I wondered how much of the fresh bear meat he'd get before the grizzlies ran him off.

"Come on cowboy. Let's get back to the ranch. They probably think we're lost."

Almost anybody can ride a horse. Abnormal fright, physical disability, or old age may keep sone folks on the ground, but by and large horseback riding is easy enough. The horses cover much more country than a man afoot. In fact, Indians claimed that a man afoot was only half a man. In big country one can see why they said this.

Your horse or mule can get you through the country and pack your gear to boot.,, Once the game is down it doesn't make much sense to plan on packing some huge animal 10 or 20 miles out to the nearest road on your back. This type of hunting is as traditional as early man. Horses have been used on all the inhabited continents over the millennia.

Let's start at the beginning. Your mount is tied to the tree, saddled and bridled. You want to get aboard and go off into the country hunting the trophy of your dreams. Before you can do this you must untie him and mount up.

The horse is tied by his lead rope. One end is tied in a slop knot to the tree and the other end is attached to his halter, the harness looking affair on his head. Over top of the halter is the bridle. The bridle is the head gear necessary to steer the horse and make him stop. The bridle holds the bit in his mouth. Two reins are attached to the bit, one for each side of the horse. Your saddle should be snug, held in place by the cinch. Your guide will take care of this. Under the saddle will be one or more saddle pads to cushion the horse form your weight. On the saddle will be a rifle scabbard and a pair of saddle bags. You will also have saddle strings to tie your jacket or whatever clothing to the back of the saddle.

The rifle scabbard may be on the right or left side of the horse. It may be fashioned to carry the rifle stock pointed forward or toward the rear of the animal. I will go over more of this later. The saddlebags are designed to carry a few small items. Your lunch, binoculars, or camera will fit into the bags. They are not designed to carry much equipment as they sit over the horse's kidneys and a heavy load here will result in a sore back for this beast of burden.

Pull the tail of the slip knot to untie the horse. Once he is untied, place each rein around his neck and let the reins sit loose and crossed on top of his neck just ahead of the saddlehorn. Holding the lead rope in one hand, now place your rifle into the scabbard. You may want to keep the magazine loaded, but never leave a shell in the chamber. Fit the rifle snugly down into the scabbard and snap the flap shut if there is one.

Now you're ready to mount. Move to the left side of the horse. This is also called the "near" side as this is the side you normally mount and dismount from. The near side is also the side the saddling and unsaddling takes place. The right side is termed as the "off" side in cowboy lingo. Most gentle horses will allow the rider to mount or dismount from either side, but you should ask your guide about this as he knows the horses. If this is as confusing as "port and starboard" forget it, and use "right and left."

Tie the lead rope around the horse's neck or simply bring the tail end of the rope back and wrap it once or twice around the saddlehorn. Allow a little belly in the rope to give the horse freedom of movement with his head and neck. Again, your guide will have his preferred method of doing this.

Take the reins in your left hand and the saddlehorn in your right. Lift your left foot into the stirrup. Now keeping your body close to the horse, lift yourself up with your right hand pulling and your left leg pushing you up. If you try this by standing out from the animal your body weight may pull the saddle off to one side. Now swing into the saddle and place your right foot in that stirrup. At this point should you find yourself looking at the horse's tail, you are backwards and must start over again.

Okay, you're up. The reins are already in your left hand and that is the hand that is best left to handling the horse. Your right hand can be used to brush away tree limbs or to hold the saddlehorn with.

Make sure the reins are even in length. It is more comfortable to place your middle finger between the reins and ride with your palm down. Your hand should be just ahead of the saddlehorn with a little belly in the reins.

Horses that neck rein, and most do, can be turned right or left by moving your left hand in that direction. Horses that plow rein will have to be pulled around by pulling his head the way you want to do. Pulling back on both reins will stop the horse. Once he is stopped further pulling will result in putting him into reverse.

Make sure your saddle is not leaning one way or the other. The saddlehorn should be straight up in line with the top of the horse's mane. Grab the horn and shift your weight which ever direction you need to adjust the saddle. You will often find that getting on moves the saddle to the left. Your rifle, because of it's weight, will sometimes want to move the saddle in that direction. Keep the saddle centered. A sore horse can't work.

To make the horse go you must kick it with your heels. If you ride with your toes pointed out and heels pointed in you will find it comfortable. Kick as you need to. Some dude horses are good travelers and some are not so good. On doggy horses you may need a switch or a lick to his butt with the tail end of the reins. Your guide will have the best remedy. Put weight into the stirrups and have your stirrups adjusted with a slight bend to your knee. It's fine to sit in the saddle. That's what it's there for, but don't plop down into it like a sack of potatoes. Your legs can help you ride. This is better for your posterior and the horse's back.

After a little practice you will find it easier and easier. Outfitters have trusty mounts. That is simply good business. No one expects you to be a bronc rider. Don't worry about the horse running off and dumping you. Your horse will follow the guide's horse. It may look like you're high up in the air, but actually it is like standing on the third step of a step ladder. You can do it. Outfitters and guides take little kids and old ladies into the mountains every summer on pack trips. They use the same horses come hunting season.

Almost everything is done at a walk. The horses travel single file where ever you go. They are trained to do this. Follow the horse ahead of you at approximately one horse length away. These are gentle horses, but a horse may not want to feel the one behind him breathing against his butt. On the other hand, don't lag behind. Your guide must communicate to you and he shouldn't have to holler to get your attention, lest he spooks the game. Then too, if you lag behind it takes longer to get where you're headed. The elk are timbered up by mid-morning. I always put it like this, "You can only go as fast as your slowest horse."

Once you're at ease and riding down the trail, you will find it amazing how nice it is just to look around. The horses add a pleasant dimension to this hunting game. Many times your horse will spot game before you do. He'll perk up his ears and look. Just look out right between his ears and you will see what he's looking at.

A guide may be guiding one or two hunters. Most hunting will be done afoot, but there is a real chance of running into game while you are riding to the spot. The hunters can take turns at being the shooter while we are mounted. The hunter directly behind me will be the shooter.

When we spot game the shooter will hand me his lead rope. I will take hold of his horse while he gets off and jerks his rifle clear of the scabbard. The shooter will quickly move out in front of the horses, chambering a round and possibly removing his scope covers. This takes up valuable time as you can see. Often times I will peel off with the horses as the shooter gets set. This saves a couple of seconds. The other hunter follows me with his horse. The shooter now has a clear field of view. As you can see, all parties have to be in tune to the plan.

At the sound of the shot the horses may bolt, but not much since we are riding them and holding them. Should we fire with the reins lying on the ground most horses run off at the sound of the shot leaving you afoot perhaps miles from camp. Old mountain horses that have been at it a good many years are used to gunfire.

I have another method that works well to get a shot if we jump game, but some hunters are reluctant to do it. I'll explain.

As you can see, it takes a little time to get set up to shoot. Some hunters are quick at getting off and ready, but unfortunately most are not. Animals don't hang around very long when you ride up on them and every second counts. For this reason I like to carry the hunter's rifle in my scabbard, on my horse. When I spot game I clear the rifle while I am still mounted. I put a round in the chamber and put it on safety while the hunter is getting off his horse. Once he hits the ground he hands me his lead rope and I hand him his rifle. The rifle is ready to go. Now the other hunter and I peel off. At the sight of game, many folks get excited. There's nothing wrong with that. This is exciting. However, your guide has been through this before and he won't be in the adrenaline rush. The guide will most likely be much quicker at getting your rifle to you than you might be yourself.

The reason some hunters don't go for this idea is that they want to carry their own rifle. After all, this rifle belongs to the hunter, and the idea of someone else carrying it doesn't set well with some hunters.

It is really not a good idea to try to carry the rifle over you shoulder while you are riding. The gun barrel sticks up and catches low branches. The rifle butt will also constantly bang against the saddle too. If you should fall from the horse the rifle will land in a pile with you, perhaps causing damage to the rifle and yourself.

The time tested rifle scabbard is the way to go. The scabbard is usually made of leather. Some scabbards are made of new synthetics that work well too. Most are designed to handle rifles with scopes. Some scabbards have a flap with a snap to prevent rain or show from getting in.

I prefer an open-ended oversized scabbard. A open-ended scabbard has no flap. Opening the flap is just one more thing to do when time is of the essence. Instead, I stuff a handkerchief into the end of the scabbard after the rifle goes in. The handkerchief acts as a wad to catch rain or snow, and it comes out quickly on it's own when I pull the rifle. If it is snowing hard and an accumulation builds up on the handkerchief, I simply pull it out and shake the snow off and replace it.

An oversized scabbard is a bit larger than usual and allows the rifle to slide in easier or to be pulled out quicker. The rifle also sets well down into the scabbard with only a few inches of the stock sticking out. The exception may be the odd rifle with a longer than usual barrel.

Don't be concerned about your rifle getting knocked off zero while it is riding around in the scabbard. If the scope is well mounted, this seldom occurs. The scabbard is adequate protection for your rifle.

When you get off your horse for any length of time, remove the rifle from the scabbard and set it down well away from any horses. The horse may lean against a tree to scratch himself and pinch the rifle between himself and the tree. Horses don't seem to give a hoot about our human possessions. To the horse your rifle is only another stick, and he sees nothing wrong with stepping on it. Horses that are hobbled or left loose to graze for a moment may also decide to roll. Imagine the scene if the rifle is on the animal at this time.

While riding along you may at some point come close to a tree that is growing right out into the trail. If it is on the same side as your rifle you could scrape up against the tree. Since the rifle is under your leg, your knee will get it first, then your rifle. There is a way around this. Rein your horse away from the tree before you get right to it. If the horse fails to respond, simply put your hand against the tree and push off from it. When you push, the horse will also move as he is part of you. This is very similar to pushing the boat away from the boat dock.

Your scabbard may be mounted on the right or left side of the horse. Guides differ on this application. Normally you get on and off on the near side of the horse. When game appears get off on whatever side the rifle is on. This will save you a run around the horse to get our rifle, again wasting time. Experienced horseback hunters jerk the rifle while they are still mounted and dismount with the rifle in hand. Most inexperienced horsemen find this difficult.

Bow hunters will find that carrying the bow while horseback is quite different from that which the rifle hunter experiences. Compound bows with sights and arrows attached do not fit well on the horse due to the size, sensitive pieces, and parts. I have seen dozens of bow scabbards, and to date I haven't found one I like. The bow needs protection above and beyond what the rifle needs. Once a scabbard is built to accommodate this you now have a piece of equipment that impedes the ability of the horse to turn, as well as putting the rider at a disadvantage to just sit comfortably in the saddle. Then too, the broadheads are attached creating the chance for a real accident. I have found a real remedy though.

Archery manufacturers build a little "S" like device that fits on your belt or hooks into your pants at the waistline. The handle of the bow rests in the bottom of the "S." This allows the hunter to rest the weight of the bow on his hip while he is walking or standing on watch. The "S" device may be made of metal or plastic, and works extremely well while riding.

When sitting on your horse the bow handle rests in the "S" again as it would otherwise. Steady the bow by placing your right hand on it. Your hip carries the weight of the bow, not your arms. When dismounting, simply step off the right side, clear of the horse. Your bow comes right with you. When mounting, hand the bow to your guide or lay it in the boughs of the tree at head high when you're standing on the ground. After you are mounted have the guide hand you the bow or ride over to the boughs and pick it up.

This system of carrying your bow also has other advantages. If trouble occurs, throw the bow clear. Believe me, you don't want to find yourself in the middle of a wreck with four or five broadheads. These arrow points work quite well on horses and people as well as game. Throwing the bow isn't as drastic as it might seem. It will probably land in the brush or weeds and be no worse for wear. Never tie the bow to the saddle or yourself for obvious reasons.

On your way into hunting camp you will probably want to pack your bow in while it's in the hard case. It will pack on the mules much the same as other cargo.

It should come as no surprise that hunters will have to ride their horses through the country in darkness. Early morning rides are necessary to get on game at daylight. Often you must wait in a good spot until the last minutes of daylight in the evening when game begins to stir. It will be dark by the time you start back, and this fact should cause no concern.

Horses, and most other animals see much better at night than we do. In addition to that they have a phenomenal sense of direction. Left to his own devices the horse will find his own way back to camp or the ranch, even in total darkness. Your horse knows where the oats are. He knows that the sooner he gets back the sooner his work day is over. In fact, the slow horse you rode out on in the morning will seem mighty energetic on the way back.

In unfamiliar country you can watch the horse sniffing his own trail back. In darkness the horse can actually feel the trail beneath his feet much the same as you would. He seldom strays from it, and has an uncanny ability to even remember logs he had to walk around in the daylight.

The guide will be riding in the lead. He will notify you of low hanging branches or other obstructions. Pay attention. A sharp stick in the eye is no fun. Refrain from shining your flashlight. The beam only blinds the horse and other people around you. If you do have to use a light, shine it upwards so only the edge of the beam illuminates the area. The sudden flicking on of an intense beam will startle many horses.

While riding at any time be aware of your various gadgets and personal gear. Stow items in deep pockets or pockets with button flaps. Notice that western shirts have flap pockets and snaps. Never carry anything in your hip pocket. The seat of your pants will slide in the saddle and your wallet or knife will come out. Guides agree that this is a bonus on the job. Since the guide rides in front, he has first chance on finding lost sporting goods. You would be amazed at the neat things I've picked up from the trail.

If you're on a horseback hunt carry a few essentials on your person at all times. If you do lose your horse you will have matches, a candy bar, and flashlight to get you back afoot. If everything is in the saddle bags it will have left with the horse.

*Horses get you there and back. They pack out the game as well.*

Pack horses and mules carry large loads of gear on their backs. A pack saddle has a rigging different from the riding saddle. There are a few types, but the difference is plain. The sacks used to place things in are called panniers. The canvas tarp that covers the load is called a pack cover or mantee. The rope that has a cinch on it is a lash rope, and this is used to tie the load down.

Horses and mules, like the rest of the animal kingdom, come in two sexes. Male horses are called stallions, but they are seldom used for this work. Stallions are proud and can become unruly in a mixed bunch of horses and mules. Castrated horses are called geldings, and geldings are commonly used.

Mares are female horses. Mares are also used frequently in this work. Be wary of riding up close behind a mare or any other horse. They may kick out at our horse, missing and hitting you instead.

Mules are hybrid animals. A mule is the result of crossing a horse on a donkey or jackass. Male mules are gelded and called John mules in most parts of the country. Female mules are called Molly mules. Mules are stronger for their size than horses, but also make good pack animals and riding animals. A mule is much smoother to ride than a horse, but it generally takes plow reining to turn him.

On a final note, let me explain how to tie up your horse. I waited until the end of this chapter because I feel it is important, and perhaps having this at the end will allow "tying" to sink in better.

Tie the animal with his lead rope, not the reins. The rope is stronger and better suited to hold the animal. Tie him high and short. By high, I mean as high as the horse's head. This prevents him from getting his head down to eat. If he gets his head down he could get a foot over the rope and find himself in a real jam. This would most likely happen after you have walked off somewhere and there would be no one around to untangle the horse for hours.

If you're tying to a tree trunk, pick a tree that will allow you to go twice around it with the rope. With two wraps pulled tightly around the tree, the rope will not wiggle down the trunk, again permitting the horse to get a leg over it. If a limb is handy, tie above the limb, and this will act as a stop to keep the rope up where it belongs.

Tie a slip knot and pull the tail of the rope through the loop for insurance that it won't come loose. Your guide may have his favorite method too, so follow his advice. Tie a horse so that there will be no question that he will be there when you return. Some guides may want to remove the bridle or loosen the clinches on the saddle. Watch and learn. If you can tie up on your own horse it saves time. You may have to dismount and walk after game. The guide can't get going until all the animals are securely tied.

Each day you're on the trail gets better and better. Riding a horse is easier than riding a bike. Soon you will wonder why you have been walking all these years.

# Trophy Care and Getting It Home
*Chapter VI*

**R**ay was an accomplished bow hunter. He had booked a 10 day hunt for moose and elk. It was September and Indian summer was in full swing. The elk were rutting and the bull moose I had scouted was also holding one cow, being in the rut as well, though it was early for the moose rut.

Ray made an excellent shot on his bull moose the first day out. The rutting bull even chased us a time or two before Ray could get a clear shot with his bow. The bull scored well enough to qualify for the Pope and Young record books.

At daylight three days later we were working a bull elk. The elk was bugling frequently above us on a timbered side hill. We tied up and cut the distance between the elk and us in half, sneaking through the dense fir and pines. Ray and I both wore full camo and head net. We knew the drill. We had gone over it in advance to save time and confusion once it began. Ray would get out in front of me. I would hide and cow call to the bull hoping he would pass by Ray while he would be searching for the cow he thought he had heard.

We set up and I called, but the bull didn't budge. I figured he might even move farther up the hill. It was a gamble, but I gave Ray a hand signal to move up. We moved quickly just in case the bull was silently headed our way. Ray and I both knew what might happen should the bull catch us flat footed in the open.

At our new position Ray was 50 yards ahead and to my left. I crouched under the low hanging boughs of a pine tree. Throwing in a couple of spike squeals got instant results. The bull bugled loudly, twice. I could hear his hooves on the ground and his antlers hitting branches as he came on. I couldn't quite see Ray as he had hidden himself behind a tree.

As if in a dream the bull elk stepped out into the open of this little clearing. I had expected him to hold to dense cover, but he caught me by surprise. He walked in long strides right at me. He would pass near enough to Ray for a shot, and I prayed that Ray was ready.

I quit calling. The bull was already coming in so fast that I didn't want to risk his breaking into a trot. If he trotted or galloped in, he could well pass Ray without the hunter being able to get a good shot. When the bull got even with Ray's position I thought about cow calling once to stop him. I decided against it, and at that moment the arrow hit the bull.

It all happened so fast. One second the bull was walking in. The next second he was hit and spinning to my left, headed back the way he had come from. The bull galloped at first. Soon he slowed to a walk, then stopped and looked back our way from over his shoulder. I saw the arrow protruding not from his pale shoulder, but from his chocolate mane. The arrow had hit him in the neck. The bull turned and walked up the hill into the trees and out of view.

Ray and I met at the center of the clearing. We whispered strained and out of breath not from the work, but from the sheer excitement of it all.

"Where did I hit him? I know I hit him."

"You hit him in the neck. You couldn't see the arrow because it was sticking out on the other side from you."

"Darn, I held on the shoulder figuring his stride would put the arrow right behind the shoulder. He heard the bow string, and turned to look just as the arrow got there. That must be why I hit him in the neck." Ray was worried. He wanted a lung hit.

I had to agree. There is a lot of meat and fur on an elk's neck. The spine or jugular vein isn't very big in comparison with the entire neck. It could well be that this would not be a mortal wound at all. The elk could heal up and go on.

We waited. In 10 minutes we heard a crash up the mountain. It was music to my ears. I knew what it meant. The bull had gone down. He was done for.

Though I was certain the bull had fallen, we took the exact route the elk had taken. It didn't take long to read the sign. Large splotches of blood turned into a small stream of blood. Ray had indeed hit the jugular vein. The bull had climbed part way up the mountain and staggered this way and that. The trail told the story. Ray led the way in the event that the bull was still alive.

I spotted him first. His antlers were caught on the base of a small pine, and his still body lay stretched down the slope. I pointed and Ray spotted his bull. What a feeling. Two trophy animals in four days, any hunter would be proud. Ray's elk was a nice five by six bull.

The ritual of hand shaking and picture taking followed. The photos are trophies in themselves and care was taken to do it right. I like to keep the sun at my back when possible to get the best photos. I removed tall blades of grass and dead branches in the foreground. Ray placed the elk facing toward me with it's legs folded underneath the large body. We wiped the blood from the bull's muzzle, and I cut the tongue out so it wouldn't flop out during the photographic session.

I had Ray sit uphill and somewhat behind the bull. This accentuates the size of the animal and it's rack. In some of the shots we laid the bow across the shoulder of the bull. The extra little things paid off in great looking pictures.

This part of the mountain side was quite steep. I went back for our horses as Ray filled out his tag. I looped the lariat over the rack and drug the bull downhill with my horse to get the animal on a level spot from which to work.

Ray wanted to have the bull mounted in a shoulder mount. He was going to have his moose done the same way. We joked about his increasing taxidermy bill. It was my job as his guide to cape out the bull and prepare the meat for the trip out of the mountains.

Ray helped with the chores. We worked and relived the episode over and over until the job was done. Ray came out the next year and took a bigger bull not 500 yards from the same spot. He brought along his nephew and that fella took his bull within a half mile of this spot. It rapidly became our lucky place. You can see why.

Trophy care is very important. The hunter spends considerable time and expense on a guided hunt. The trophy animal is the icing on the cake, and all care must be given to make sure the trophy is in good shape for the taxidermist.

A shoulder wall mount is undoubtedly the most popular way of displaying the trophy head on horned and antlered animals. Sometimes the hunter wants a full body mount. This may be more common with sheep and goats than it is with large animals like elk. More rarely, a hunter will want a half mount. This is where the front half of the animal appears to be coming out of the wall.

European mounts are the bleached skulls of the animals. Inexpensive, but still attractive, European mounts are becoming increasingly more popular. Bear and mountain lion skulls are routinely bleached as they are used in measuring trophy status for the record books. The hides of these two animals are normally considered the trophy, and they are usually life-sized or rugged. Bear and lion heads are mounted too, but not often.

The diagrams should be explanatory, showing the necessary cuts to make. It is the guide's job to perform these tasks, although every hunter should have a working knowledge of these skinning chores.

When skinning, pull the hide with one hand while cutting the hide from the meat with the other. A sharp knife is essential and one should always have a sharpener or stone with him. An axe, hatchet, or saw may be used for cutting bone. If you know where the joints are however, you can get by with a knife everywhere except removing the skull plate from the skull. Knives come in every style imaginable. I prefer a smaller knife with a straight point or a dropped point.

Never pull the blade toward yourself. A slip here might result in pulling the blade into you. Every year some unlucky hunter cuts his own femoral artery and bleeds to death in the field. Carry bandaids in your pocket for any small cuts to your fingers.

Let's now get into some handy tips for handling different animals.

Horned and antlered game must have the skin removed at the hairline where the base of the horns begins. One diagonal cut is made toward the backside of each horn from the main cut that stops at the backside of the skull. This forms a "Y" looking affair, one cut up the back of the neck, stopping at the backside of the skull, then one cut up to the base of each horn.

The next cut is one that rings the skin around the horn right at the hairline. To loosen the skin around the boney base, you can skin along with your knife. I prefer to use a stubby little slot screwdriver with a slight bend in the blade. With this tool I can jam it in along the base loosening the hide as I go. Some knife work is still required, but this speeds up the process. The hide at the base of the horns is very thick and not likely to rip.

When skinning out the face you roll the skin inside out as you go. It is very similar to grabbing your sock at the top and peeling it down your ankle and off your foot. Care must be taken around the eyes and lips to make sure you get all the skin. The nose has plenty of cartilage, and simply leave the cartilage in at this point to be cleaned out later.

*Caping a bull Moose*

When skinning for rugs or life-sized mounts, we need to keep the legs and the feet or hooves. Bear paws and the hooves of horned game can be skinned out in camp where it is more comfortable and where you have a better work place. In the field you can wring the wrist or ankle bones off leaving the foot intact. If you have trouble finding the joint you can chop the leg bone with an axe or saw it off. If an axe is used, place a good sized stick underneath the bone before you hit it. Wedge the stick between the skin and bone and pull the hide back from the stick so you don't cut the hide with the axe. The stick gives you something solid under the bone to aid in cracking it more easily.

There is an important trick to skinning out the front legs of animals that are to be rugs. Make your cut from the center of the throat at the little hollow point at the top of the chest. Don't start out along the arms from the center of the chest. Cut along the top of the arms, not the inside. If you do this right the rug will have good width along the body. If you do it wrong you will have a flap of skin that is attached to the shoulder when it should be attached to the flank. The taxidermist must cut this flap off and resew it to the side of the skin where the underarm meets the side of the animal. Some taxidermists may just cut it off and discard it, leaving you with an hour glass looking rug.

Unless you're able to freeze the skin before it spoils it should have the ears and lips turned and salt applied liberally to the fleshy side.

Turning the ears means cutting between the cartilage and the skin on the backside of the ear. Skin right up to the tip of the ear. And turn it inside out. The lips are full of small muscles, and this meat will spoil unless you split the lips from the inside of the hide. When these two tasks are complete, pack the areas with salt and re-close them.

The hide should be removed of fat and meat, then salted using as much salt as you can. When this is completed, roll it up fur side out, with the head on the inside of the roll. After salting, the hide will leak water. The salt leaches out fluids and the entire hide may become soggy until the fluids are gone. Salting prevents bacteria from starting the rotting process. Always use non-iodized salt. This salt allows for a better tanning process.

If it is cool outdoors your hide will keep to some degree without salt if it is rolled up. Heat and direct sunlight are the enemies of raw skins. A cool shady place with a good air flow is best for storing. If you want to place the skin in something, use a cloth pillow case or burlap feed sack, whatever is at hand. Don't use a plastic garbage sack. The plastic holds in heat and does

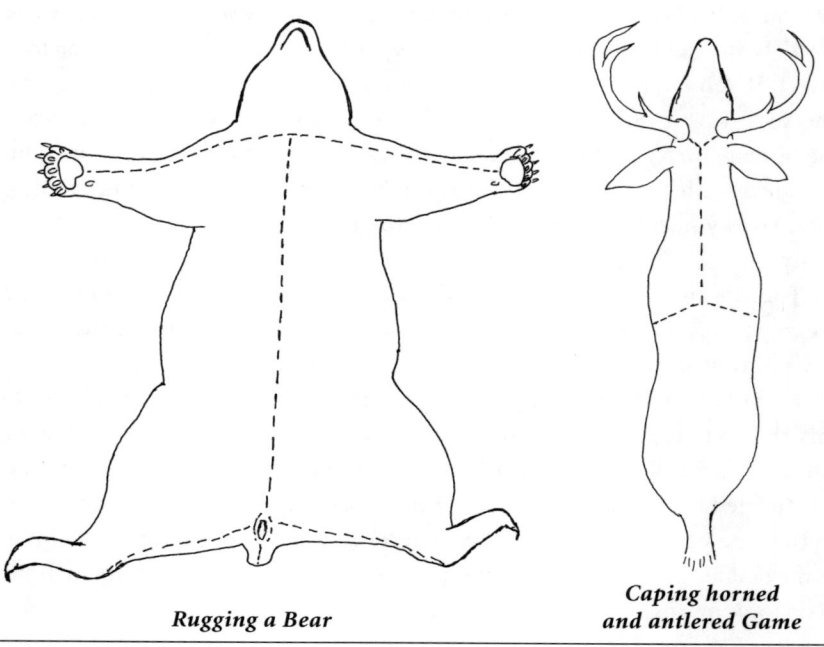

*Rugging a Bear*

*Caping horned and antlered Game*

not allow air flow. In warm weather it is good to cover the skin to keep files from laying their eggs on it. Here too, salt keeps the flies off.

Everything seems to go at a faster pace these days. As a result, freezing is often used to keep skin in good shape for the trip home. When you get to town find a cardboard box that will accommodate the hide. In this case you can line the box with double plastic trash bags. Place the rolled up hide in the box and leave it open at the top. Place the box in the freezer. The open box will let warm air out and cold air in. The hide freezes in a nice cube inside the box. It is very difficult to place a hard round hide in a square box. Seal the bags and tape the box shut. This package will keep well enough for the trip home. Go to the taxidermist immediately or place the box in your freezer at home. Here again, it is easy to see why you should plan on a full day after the hunt before you depart for home.

Before I go on too far I want to hit on problem hides. These are unusual things, but you should be aware of them.

For some reason bear hides will slip, or rot much quicker than most other animals. I am told that it is due to enzymes in the fat, I don't know. All precautions must be taken with a bear.

Moose and antelope each have a feature that needs attention. The bell on the moose is a hollow tube of skin. This tube should be split open to allow air in or opened to get salt into it. If the bell is not opened it may well rot. Antelope have a double layer of skin on the side of the face. You can salt the face, but unless this double layer is opened from the inside, this too will rot.

The tail bone of all animals should be removed, and the tail split open for the same reasons. Even the smallest of tails require this.

The airlines have rules about accepting your set of antlers for airline travel. The meat and skins are easy. These go in boxes as extra baggage. Large sets of antlers will not fit into boxes. Small sets may be sawed in two at the skull, but larger trophy sets are often sent home on the plane in one piece. The airlines do not permit antlers to be carried on as "carry on" baggage. The rack must go in as cargo.

To meet airline specs is easy enough though and not to worry. Cover each tip with a piece of hose. Garden hose or automobile heater hoses work well. Use duct tape to wrap the hose on the tips, and don't be afraid to use too much. The skull must be wrapped so no blood will leak and no meat or bone is exposed to upset the non-hunting public. I like to wrap it in cloth, then plastic, and lastly more duct tape. The "friendly sky folks" also want a brace spanning across the rack to keep the two antlers from collapsing together. A one-by-two, or dowel rod works well. Tape it into place after you have wedged it in halfway up the antlers.

Place two extra info tags on the antlers. The airlines will place another one on at your time of departure too. The tags will have your name, address, flight number, and destination. If one tag comes off you will still have two more working for you. I have not, to date, seen any antlers turn up missing or damaged this way.

*Elk Antlers ready for travel*

You may opt to use a taxidermist in your own hometown, or one located near your hunting. If you choose a taxidermist in Backwoods, USA, or Lost Mountain, Canada, he is sure to be familiar with the type of game animals in his neck of the woods. At times the outfitter may recommend a local taxidermist. This may be easier than getting your trophy home after the hunt, but make sure you understand the shipping arrangements after the trophy is mounted.

Remember that once the trophy is taken to the taxidermist, the outfitter should not be put in the position of middleman. He is not a taxidermist, and many outfitters don't want to baby-sit heads all year.

Taxidermists may tan their skins in their shop or send them out to a tannery. A taxidermist who has a large volume of work often uses the tannery. Big tanneries do quality work to be sure. It might also be that your hide will get lost or damaged at the tannery. This doesn't happen often, but it happens. If need be, offer to pay extra if the taxidermist is able to tan it in his shop.

Sometimes the head is brought out of the hills before it is fully caped. It may be that the head must be tied to a pack horse, four wheeler, or snowmobile. If this is the case, never tie a rope across the bridge of the animal's nose. The hair is short on the animal's face. If the rope cuts the hairs it is almost impossible to repair this properly. You wouldn't want a mounted head with a rope burn across the nose.

Game meat is usually handled in the town where the outfitter is located. Hunting towns almost always have several reliable butchers who know how to package meat for shipment. Take their advice on these details. The butcher will have shipping boxes and dry ice. One word of caution... Butchers are not fond of being rushed because your plane is supposed to leave in the next two hours. Give him time to do his job.

In warm weather hunters run the risk of meat spoilage. Your outfitter will see to it that the meat is taken out. In the mean time there is a trick that I learned from a butcher to keep the flies off your meat. Sprinkle black pepper liberally over exposed meat. There are also some commercial products available just for this. Flies lay their eggs on meat. Fly eggs left to hatch become what?

Your guide should be able to handle trophies and meat in the field. This is part of his job description. I like to make a little party out of the work. Open up the lunches and build a fire. This only an unpleasant job when everyone gets in a hurry.

*The End Result!*

# Being Prepared
*Chapter VII*

**G**.W. and I were hunting mule deer and antelope. I was guiding him on a five day hunt, commonly termed as a combination hunt. A combination hunt can work well in some areas, but often you'll find that you can't really apply yourself totally to hunting either animal. In this case hunter and guide can only hit the high spots due to a short time period.

G.W. had booked the hunt late for whatever reason, and the outfitter hired me on the spur of the moment. I knew the country though. These were rolling hills, where the mountains gradually broke off into prairie. It was November and the mule deer were coming down from the mountains to get onto their winter range. The antelope lived here full time, but some of the antelope bucks were beginning to shed their horns.

I met G.W. the night before the hunt in his motel room. He was a nervous wreck, but I was really taken with the mountain of gear sprawled out on his bed. While we talked I kept staring at this pile of clothing and sporting goods.

"Randy, I want a big buck and a big antelope."

Actually, both male deer and antelope are termed as bucks, but I knew what he meant.

"Well, that's what we're here for. We'll be huntin' some good country. Did you shoot earlier today while you were with Tom?"

"No, we ran out of time. My gun's on though. What time you gonna pick me up in the morning?"

"I'll pick you up here at a quarter to five. We'll get breakfast at the cafe and head out."

As you might guess, I was getting a bad feeling already. This guy was in a big rush and demanded big animals. G.W. lived in the fast lane in his everyday life. It would have been nice if he relaxed and enjoyed the hunt, but in reality I didn't figure him for the relaxing type. Keeping a stiff upper lip is yet another trait required to be a guide.

That night four inches of heavy wet snow fell silently over the entire countryside. I knew that this would mean another muddy day. "Gumbo" is aptly named. The sticky mud piles up on the tires to the point of clogging the wheel wells. It accumulates on a man's boots until each foot weighs twenty pounds. In the dark of morning I was so worried about the gumbo that I barely noticed the fog.

I picked up G.W. in the gloom of night, determined to keep to my appointed round. I waited in the pickup as he kept going back to his room for more stuff. With each trip I would offer to help, but he declined the offer only to go back in for more. Soon the cab was filled up and he started loading the bed. Finally he jumped in and slammed the door shut behind him.

"Okay guide, let's hit it."

I turned into the parking lot at the cafe when he shouted, "Wait, go back, I forgot something."

Go back we did. G.W. ran into the room and came out in a rush, slamming the door of the pickup again.

"We better skip breakfast. Let's go."

I really didn't mind missing my breakfast at G.W.'s insistence, but I wasn't about to miss my morning coffee. I stopped at the convenience store and picked up two large coffees to go. I got the big ones in the styrofoam cups with the plastic lids. Trying to be polite, I popped the little tab for G.W., and he placed his cup on the dash. He rummaged around with his gear as we passed under the street lights. By the time we got out on the highway he was wearing his binoculars, shell belt, sheath knife, and the rest. He had barely put a dent in the pile. The windshield wipers clapped time to the cassette cowboy tunes and a light rain now mixed with the heavy fog.

I turned off onto a county road and G.W.'s coffee tipped over and ran down into the defroster. I had the wrong attitude. I had to turn this around.

"You got a lot of stuff there G.W.," I said in a lighthearted voice.

"Yea, I go prepared. I got two of everything. You never know. That's why I have two backpacks in the bed. One's for deer and one's for antelope. Hey, that reminds me, they're getting wet back there. We better pull over so I can bring them up front."

Now the pile between us prevented us from even seeing each other. What could he possibly have in all of this stuff? I turned off onto the dirt two track road, and as I suspected, the gumbo bogged us down. I pulled down into four-wheel-drive and chugged along.

"How long you been huntin' G.W.?"

"Really, I've only been at a couple of years, but my buddies say I'm the luckiest guy they've ever seen. Just this year I killed a good bull elk in Montana, and a mule deer in Idaho. After this hunt I'm goin' up to Saskatchewan to hunt whitetails. I got a big one up there last year. But, before I go there, I'm going back home to hunt whitetails on my own place. I bought a farm, and I got a good buck there last year too.

"This stuff I got here, well, I find I need something else on every hunt I go on."

It was hard to believe. I had guided several hunters who had hunted all over the place year after year. Those guys though were quite professional in their manner having a good deal of experience under their belt, so to speak. G.W., on the other hand, acted pretty green to have that amount of kills in such a short period of time.

"Whad a ya do for a livin' G.W.?"

"I did good in real estate, and I bought a sporting goods store a few years ago."

I should have guessed. Everyone goes through the gadget stage at some time or another. It was easy to see how a sporting goods merchant would naturally fall into this in a big way. I spun off the two track to avoid a good-sized pothole. I wheeled out into the sagebrush slinging mud up over the hood when, Pow! The right tire blew. Air rushed out for a second or two, then nothing.

The countryside was getting gray as G.W. and I got out to assess the damage. I had run over a broken off steel post. The tire was ruined. I couldn't believe my bad luck. Nothing was going right. Fog engulfed us and the good hunting country was still two miles away. It was getting daylight, and here we sat with a flat.

I dug the handyman jack from out of the tool box. Luckily the spare had air in it, and I consoled myself thinking it might only slow us up 30 minutes or so. The jack sunk into the mud and slid sideways despite my best efforts. I jumped up into the bed to look for a board or something I could place under the jack.

"I got one of those little floor jacks in the trunk of my rental car back in town. I bought it when I rented the car. I knew we should have brought it with us." G.W. walked around the truck as he spoke, looking for more flat tires.

I was ready to scream. "G.W. get your rifle and walk over there and look for some deer while I get this tire changed." I pointed through the fog toward the faint outline of a rise in the prairie.

You could barely see 30 yards and the deer hunting was still two miles away, but being mean spirited, I sent him away. As I worked I felt a little bad about it. It wasn't his fault. This was just hunting. This was just one of those bad days.

I lowered the truck down from the jack and the new tire looked pretty good. I rolled the ruined tire into the bed thinking about the dollar signs, and decided to put it out of my mind. Pulling back onto the two track I sat behind the wheel wondering where all that coffee went to in the heater. I wondered if it would come out somewhere, when I heard a shot.

Oh no. I knew better than to leave him alone. It was my fault. I knew better. His gun went off. Oh God, I hope he's all right. I jumped out of the truck and ran toward the rise. I slipped and slid in the mud and snow. I had had so much bad luck that I simply assumed it was a permanent condition. It was becoming a complex. In my mind it was I I I, me me me.

"G.W. Where are you? ....G.W. Where are you?"

"I'm over here.... I got a deeeeeeeeer."

No, it couldn't be true. There were no deer here. They were farther up toward the mountain. Was this some kind of a dream or what? I found him sitting beside his buck fumbling in his "deer pack" with stuff scattered around him in the snow.

And a buck it was. The rack was only 24 inches or so, but he had heavy dark horns with four points on each side and brow tines like a side order of fries. There was no story to it. G.W. had walked over the rise and ran smack into the grazing buck. The deer looked up at him through the fog, and never even spooked. G.W. took him with one shot behind the shoulder. There was a God.

"Boy, you're some guide. You knew right where to go. Tom said you would. I worried you might not know, but you did." He went on and on.

With each slap on the back it felt more and more like a blow from a sledge. I hadn't given G.W. much credit. He seemed like a greenhorn. I had been thinking of my own predicament so much I had forgotten why I was there.

Humility is a wondrous thing.

I gladly helped G.W. set up his camera with the tripod on it. He had a spotting scope with a tripod too. Scattered around were a space blanket, dried food packages, rope, two boxes of shells, extra film, first aid kit, thermos bottle, extra gloves, flashlight, extra batteries, a fire starter kit, a knife sharpening kit, compass, and some kind of a contraption that would hoist a deer into a tree.

Yes, G.W. had quite a deer pack. He later informed me that in the side pockets he also had maps, toilet paper, a fold up cup, twine, and a survival book in paperback form. I didn't care. He had a buck down on the snow when all things were against us. G.W. carried his rifle and deer pack while I drug the buck that hung up on every sagebrush we ran into.

"Randy, I have all kinds of stuff to drag a deer with. You want to try some of this stuff?"

"No thanks G.W. I can get the truck up here. You wait with your deer, and I'll go get the truck."

We went to Tom's house with the deer. G.W. jumped out even before I got all the way stopped and started bending Tom's ear about the deer and his Davey Crockett guide. Tom was all smiles. The outfitter loves it when his clients get game. Tom especially liked this since he didn't have to be there. G.W. was cluing Tom in on the finer points of deer hunting when Tom waved me off to get my tire fixed. At noon the first day of the hunt we had it half over. I made a pact with myself to give G.W. my best effort on his antelope hunt.

The stars were bright the next morning when I pulled into the motel. G.W. was waiting outside holding his little floor jack. He threw it in the bed with a loud clang, and we headed off again without breakfast. We were down to one pack now and things were looking up.

God watches over children, drunks, and G.W. He knocked down the first antelope buck he shot at. We had spotted two that we couldn't' get on at first. Then we ran into this one as I was driving to a new spot. G.W. bailed out and had him down while I was still trying to pull off the two track. This 14 incher sacrificed himself to become G.W.'s first antelope.

Happily we were handling the antelope, and I was explaining to G.W. how I thought an antelope makes the prettiest mount, when the left horn popped off. G.W. stood holding the horn in his hand with his mouth hanging open, speechless. He looked like a kid who had just broken a flower vase.

"What the hell is this?"

I laughed, "He was just about to shed his horns. If you pull on the other one it'll probably come off too."

"Well that aint' right," G.W. didn't look amused. "I'm gonna' write a letter to the Game and Fish. This is a hell of a way to do things."

I talked until I was blue in the face about shedding horns and the time of year. Finally G.W. said he had a book on antelope and he would read up on this. I assured him his taxidermist would take care of everything.

G.W. left in a hurry, the same way he arrived. His deer and antelope weren't at the butchers yet, but he gave Tom a wad of money to cover it all. Tom would ship his meat and have the taxidermy done right here in town. We waved good-bye as he backed down the driveway.

G.W. hollered out the window as he turned onto the street, "Keep my floor jack. You'll need it."

I had forgotten it was in the back of my truck. We waved, and he was gone.

Being prepared for the hunt can mean many things. It is true that one needs the proper gear. However, there is more to it than that. Gear cannot make up for real hunting. One has little chance in relying on luck, hoping the guide or the sporting goods will bet it done. Hunting requires patience, skill, and sometimes physical endurance. The work makes the event rewarding.

It takes a tremendous amount of patience for some folks to sit for hours on a stand. This is necessary though to get a shot at many types of game. Bow hunters seem to have that patience, or they soon give it up. Bow hunters most generally evolve into the sport after first being a rifle hunter.

When I was a kid I learned to sit my butt down and wait the hard way. The deer were always running out ahead of me and I seldom saw much of the fleeing deer, let alone get a good shot. My dad sat still and killed consistently. I should have quickly learned by example. A kid is fidgety by nature though, and it took some time for me to settle down.

One way to learn patience is to take along a book to read. Read a couple of pages and look around. Read a couple of more and look some more. It works. While you read, your mind rests from the task at hand. While reading, you will notice that you move your body less also. Body movement is the normal culprit when an animal spots you. It is a good idea to look around at each flip of the page.

Patience is definitely an acquired skill. Those hunters who are best at it are hunters who have scored on trophy animals while in wait. Any style of hunting that gets results soon becomes a favorite. Confidence grows, and waiting begins to have other rewards as well.

While on a stand things slow down. You notice each rock or tree individually. It doesn't take long to be very familiar with your surroundings at a full 360 degrees. You begin to visualize the animal even before he approaches. This is good.

Visualize all of the possible avenues an animal might approach long before it happens. Ask yourself what would you do if he showed here, or there? Will you be ready? Are you waiting in the right place? Go over every detail. This process alone will chase the boredom away.

I don't look at waiting as if it were work. I admit I hate to wait on people. It drives me crazy. Waiting on game can be taken to an art form. I can outwait that rock. I can be that rock. When the bear comes I'll have waited to the point I even look like that rock. With this attitude, things like that can and do happen too. Squirrels and other small animals and birds sometimes try to sit on you. Thus, another hunting bonus is born.

Animals are not in a hurry. They have no timetables except to eat and sleep. Time means little and they go easy, not wanting to call attention to themselves. It is the most elementary of survival tricks. A cow elk can stand motionless and stare at the edge of the meadow for 20 minutes before she commits to come out and feed.

When I'm guiding a hunter, I try to sit beside, and slightly behind him. This gives him a clear field of view, and I am close enough to whisper things to him if I have to. It works well, but occasionally it works against us. Naturally enough, we may get to talking. Before you know it we are making too much noise. In this case I move back away from him. If I need to get his attention I might throw a pebble his way, or a pine cone to alert him to something.

Here is a word of caution concerning the waiting game. Never set your rifle or bow down and sit yourself down beyond easy reach of it. I have seen this happen too many times. The hunter assumes wrongly that he can get to it with no problem. There is a problem though. The animal generally spots him reaching and catches the hunter flat footed. Keep your weapon close always.

Sitting on a stand doesn't conjure up the glamour of tracking or stalking, but nearly everyone agrees most game is gotten this way. Whitetail deer hunters who I guide are the best at it. Some of these guys figure they are not hunting unless they are on a stand.

Tracking game down and bagging the same is difficult for a guide and hunter. Animals tend to watch their back trail. Again, this is another survival trait. Wounded game especially does this. Tracking works though, and many hunters are not that well versed in it.

Tracking in the snow is easy enough. Tracking on hard, broken ground comes only from doing plenty of it. Entire books have been written on tracking. I find the stories about tracking dangerous game very entertaining. Man tracking would be the ultimate, but I am getting off the subject. Tracking not only requires an eye on the ground, but another eye on your surroundings to spot the animal before it flees.

While I'm tracking game I like to keep the hunter right at my heels. This way I can point or use other hand signals rather than talking. Since I am in the lead the spore is fresh and unspoiled. Many times it is only a small portion of the track one can see. Since I am in the front I can pick out places to put my feet down to keep noise to a minimum. The hunter can place his feet exactly where mine had just been. Two hunters can move quietly this way. Stealth is of the utmost importance.

My nose is in the track most of the time. It is necessary to keep my concentration on the trail and the animals movements. The hunter should be watching ahead, and to each side. A good hunter looks for part of an animal rather than the whole critter. A leg or patch of fur is often the only visible sighting at first.

When my hunter spots something he only has to tap my shoulder. If we are in sync I can drop to my knees and freeze. This gives the hunter a better look should the animal be out front. It is a good idea to have the hunter move right up in front of the guide as the guide kneels. If these moves are done in unison it works pretty slick.

Hunters should carry their rifles at port arms during this tracking game. The time and extra movement it takes to get the gun ready can hurt you. Never carry the rifle pointed at the guide or anyone else. If the rifle becomes heavy simply carry it in the crook of your arm. I have turned to say something to the hunter only to find myself looking down the barrel. It sure takes the fun out of things.

Hard soled boots are not my favorite for sneaking around. Those big lug soles break small sticks and the toe often bangs loudly into rocks or logs. It seems that the colder it gets outside the harder these soles become. Soft sole boots allow you to kind of feel the ground before the weight comes down. The soft sole bends over many sticks rather than breaking them.

Soft clothing also brushes against things quietly. With the amount of outdoor clothing available it is easy to find something that fits the bill. Most rainwear is noisy, but many types of quiet, warm clothing adorn the pages of mail order catalogues.

After the shot it is sometimes that more tracking is in order. This is usually the case in arrow hit animals. It doesn't matter to me where it is hit. I want 30 minutes for the arrowhead to do its work. Believe me when I say this amount of time seems like an eternity. The suspense is nerve wracking while the hunter grabs the guide's collar and demands to go. Now!

Bleeding animals are not as easy to track as some might think. After the hit they are in a panic. The animal may bound away in 20 foot jumps, leaving only four bunched up tracks in a small place. Animals can jump sideways too. They will sometimes backtrack. They may go uphill or down. The old wives tale about wounded animals traveling downhill is not reliable. Wounded game may keep to the cover or even strike out across open country. It is best to expect the unexpected.

It is a bad idea to second guess animals while you're tracking them. I was becoming a fairly good tracker at a young age. I even became a little cocky about it. I figured I could "head 'em off at the pass." It never did work well. This only slowed the tracking down and I lost time. Stay on the trail.

Blood dries more quickly than you might think. Dried blood stays red for awhile, but it doesn't shine like wet blood. Blood might only be a single, lonely drop at a time. Much of it may stick to the animal's fur like a sponge. This is true of bears especially. Look high on branches and leaves on the branches. Blood will stick here as the animal moves through the brush. You may even find more of it up on things than you do on the ground.

I once guided a hunter who was color blind. He could see wet blood, but had a difficult time seeing dried blood. I pointed to blood on a sandstone rock and he couldn't see it. I have a tough time seeing day-old blood in some cases. Much of it becomes brown and blends into the surroundings.

Losing the trail is common. In this case stop dead in your tracks and look about slowly. Look behind you and find the last two places you saw blood, Next turn facing forward and draw an imaginary line using the last two places. This rule of thumb will put you back on the animal's line of travel. It isn't foolproof, but it works more often than not.

Approaching darkness, rain, and snowfall might threaten the tracking process. It happens. Don't get in a hurry. Being frantic on the track is far worse than the elements.

Two sets of eyes are better than one. If the hunter is watching, he will spot the downed game before the guide, who has his nose to the ground, steps on it. Wounded animals can be dangerous. The hunter should always be ready.

Notice the last sentence was, "the hunter should always be ready." This is what I meant when I titled this chapter "Being Prepared." There is more to being prepared than meets the eye. Not every hunt turns out like G.W.'s hunt. More work and knowledge is almost always necessary.

"Work." None of us like it, but sometimes work becomes play. Having a good time is at the head of the hunter's list and a good hunter will work at it. You must be in shape.

Walking and jogging are common means of exercise. Walking is what we do when we hunt so it would make sense to walk before you go on the hunt. Walking takes time, and time is a luxury these days, I know. Nevertheless, exercising is important, as is shooting. Both things are needed on the hunt. Get in shape at home. It's your hunt.

You might have noticed that I keep avoiding all the equipment you'll need. I avoid rifle calibers, and bows, and arrows too. There is so much out there that it would take volumes to write about it. Many items become obsolete in short order these days too. There is one area that many hunters are confused about though, and that is the question of optics. Optics change as everything else, but there are basic things to consider.

Rifle scopes, binoculars, and spotting scopes are commonly used when we speak of hunting optics. I hope that heat seeking, night vision, molecular stuff can wait for future generations, or forever. There are hundreds of types of optics out there. You get what you pay for, but even so, I feel many are overpriced.

We want magnification and clarity. We want optics that gather light in the early dawn and late evening. We want looking glasses that show little heat distortion on warm days or long distances. We want things to look through that don't shake around in our hands, making it impossible to focus. And speaking of focus, we want it, and we want it quick.

Rifle scope come in variable power scopes and fixed power scopes. A variable scope will magnify at a lower power and increase the magnification higher and higher as you turn the dial. These variables used to be considered less clear than fixed power scopes, but it is hard to tell today. They are still generally heavier in weight than a fixed power, but that too is changing.

Fixed power scopes are of the old adage, "what you see is what you get." These scope give you one setting. Fixed power scopes are simple since they have no dials to manipulate. They can be of any magnification, but usually they are lighter and more compact than the variable models.

The sights inside the scope also cover a wide range of choices. Plain cross hairs, fat cross hairs that grow slimmer as they cross at the center, cross hairs with a dot in the middle, range finder cross hairs that have a series of crosses for different ranges, and cross hairs that have a post called a command post. There are others too, but these are the more common garden varieties.

It is not an easy choice deciding which type to go with. I prefer a medium thickness cross hair, Fine cross hairs seem to disappear in low light. Heavy cross hairs cover up too much target area at longer ranges.

If I were to choose which magnification were best I would choose a straight six power fixed scope or a three to nine power variable. Two to four power settings do not magnify the target much at longer ranges. Scopes that are, say 10 or 12 power, need to be held extremely still to focus on the target. You may notice that in the sporting goods store or mail order catalogue these two types I have mentioned are the most common. That is simply because most hunters find straight sixes and three to nines their favorites also.

Never point a gun in any direction you do not intend to shoot. Fathers have taught their sons this for many years. Gun clubs do the same. It is, of course, good advice. Your rifle is mounted with a rifle scope, and that scope is one more optic at your disposal. Is it safe to use your scope to spot game? Some would say no.

I feel that if the hunter is certain that there is not a round in the chamber he is not being unsafe by using his scope to look across the canyon at some object that catches his eye. In the back country at least, buildings, farm animals, and other people are few and far between. It may be unreasonable otherwise, but at some point we have to accept the fact that people can make the distinction between what is safe and what is not.

Why not just use your binoculars? This is a good point. After all, those binoculars around your neck can't go off by accident.

When someone hands you a shotgun you first check to make sure it is unloaded. Then you bring it to your shoulder and point it at the sky looking down the barrel. You hand the gun back to the fellow and that's that. When someone hands you a scoped rifle you check it. He says, "Go ahead, look through it." You pick a safe direction and look through the scope. You don't point it at the sky because you'll see nothing. You point the scoped rifle at something. Is this unsafe? We do it all the time. Is pointing the rifle at something in the field any different? Okay, I'm building up to something.

A hunter who never looks through his scope, except on the rare occasion when game shows up, may have a hard time even finding the animal in the scope because he is not familiar with handling his rifle. He may be all right if he shoots at the range a great deal, but otherwise he is usually slow and hesitant. Add a little adrenaline at the moment of truth and this problem magnifies itself even more. Relying on the binoculars every time gives one no practical experience with the rifle. Again, we have the capability to be responsible people. Even if the nation seems to be slipping into mediocrity, does that mean that no one can be considered competent?

Binoculars or field glasses are a great hunting aid, and I recommend them as part of your gear for your guided hunt. Like rifle scopes there are a thousand different models and makes to choose from. Large, 20 power sets are good for looking at far off objects, but they are heavy to carry and generally require a rest to get a look at something to keep the natural shake of your body from distorting the view.

Compact classes are popular these days. They are small and easy to stick in your pocket. They come in a wide range of magnification, and the better brands are quite clear. I find that small binoculars catch my breath faster in cold weather. By this I mean that the eyepieces fog up from my breath due to the design. I can't put my finger on it, but medium sized glasses don't seem to do this.

Medium sized glasses are just that. Around two pounds in weight, and six to eight inches in length, this is the size your dad had when you were a kid. With the improvements in today's glasses that may be the only similarity.

Seven or ten power glasses are most popular for hunting purposes. Compact or medium sized glasses have fast focus and varying fields of view. Ten power glasses seem to be outpacing the sevens, but a steady hand is needed for long scrutiny of objects because of the higher magnification.

I like binoculars that have the rubber coating over the outside of the entire unit. The dull finish on these rubberized glasses doesn't give off a glare when the sunlight hits them. This could alarm an animal to your presence. The coating also prevents a ticking sound when an object hits against the glasses in the case of hard plastic, or a tinkling sound in the case of metal exteriors. Setting the rubberized versions down on a rock or log, you will find that they kind of grip it. They are not as apt to slide off as hard surfaced glasses might.

While guiding hunters in all types of conditions I prefer to use ten power, compact, rubber coated binoculars. The only draw back I've found is that mules like them too. I once had a mule chew a set of these into pieces. I think he liked the chewy rubber, and when he finished the remnants lay on the ground. The glasses had a wonderful manufacturers warranty, but I couldn't bring myself to test it.

Spotting scopes are usually found in variable powers, though fixed power scopes are on the market. The spotting scope is used for scanning the country for miles around. If game is spotted you can turn up the magnification and judge the size of the animal, even miles away.

On the low end of the magnification table 15 power is good. Remember that you have nearly that with your binoculars or rifle scope. On the high end of the magnification 30 or 35 is adequate. Some scopes go up to 60 power, but heat distortion in the air currents makes the big 60s difficult to use.

Spotting scopes are commonly used on small compact tripods for stability while glassing. These tripods have retractable legs and the scope screws down onto the mount on the tripod. Many times I simply use a rock to scope from, holding one hand down firmly on top of the scope to steady it.

If you find yourself hunting open country from a vehicle you may want to use a window mount. This mount clamps down on your car window. Roll the window up or down for the proper height while you sit behind the wheel. A little handle on the mount allows you to rotate the scope around on the mount.

Long days spent behind the lens may leave you with a headache from eye strain. This is normal, even for folks with good vision. Carry aspirin to relieve this condition. To help prevent eye strain use a patch over your other eye. A hunter I once guided showed me this trick, and it works.

One type of hunting aid that may or may not be considered as optics is a range finder. Archery hunters picked up on it first. You look through the eye piece and focus on an object. The little gadget then shows you a number indicating the yardage. The early models were good for 60 yards or less. Archery hunters would focus on objects around their stand to identify various distances. When game showed up you only had to remember the different objects and their distances. Is this critter standing near that 20 yard log, or that 35 yard stump?

Recently a hunter gave me a peek through the new and improved version. The range finder hung around his neck like a good sized pair of binoculars. It was battery operated and recorded ranges of up to one thousand yards. We had quite a time guessing at ranges, while focusing on this or that. This thing is a real learning tool, but it is a considerable amount to carry if you have other equipment as well. I believe this type of range finder would really shine at the rifle range where one must know his various distances to determine rifle performance.

The more knowledge you collect on your own, the better prepared you will be. That is the bottom line. Application of knowledge will only come with experience.

*Being prepared surely makes a difference.*

# Some Hunting Tricks That Work
*Chapter VIII*

Who among us hasn't gazed into the night sky? On a clear night the stars shine pure and primal. I have seen Orion in the night sky. The constellation Orion, the hunter, are some of the brightest stars in the sky. I have seen Orion here on earth too. His name was Martin, and I was his guide while we hunted mule deer on a frozen mountain side in mid-November.

The rut was beginning and an even foot of snow blanketed the slope. Snow laid heavy too, on the pine bows waiting for a Chinook wind to blow it to the ground. In the bitter cold the powder squeaked beneath our boots. Our lungs burned hiking across the frigid face of the mountain looking for a truly big buck. I was a young guide at the time, and it was to my consternation and eventual delight that Martin would settle for nothing less.

I was sent by my boss to pick up our hunter at the Billings airport. Martin filed off the plane with other hunters bound for all points of Montana and Wyoming. He was in his mid-30s I'd say. Slight of build and not that tall, he had a quiet, sharp look about him. Martin picked up his one medium-sized duffle and rifle case before we left the airport. My rookie eyes picked up on the wear and tear of his meager luggage. It was to be my first clue that Martin himself was no rookie.

During the drive back to Cody we chatted. Martin was shooting a .30-06 with hand-loaded rounds. When he claimed that he had taken 21 trophy mule deer bucks I must have looked skeptical. Him, being from New York and all. He then went on to explain that he only hunted deer and nothing else. For several years he'd hunted no less than five Rocky Mountain states each season. He had invented and patented some gadget that now paid royalties, hence his life-style. Still an hour from town, I grew quiet measuring myself against all of his previous guides. A lump settled nicely in my throat.

Back at the ranch I tentatively asked the boss why he had picked me to guide this guy. A couple of my fellow guides had scored on far more game than I had. I figured that this must be some kind of a mistake or something.

Butch laid it out straight as usual. "Look, this guy is a "walker." He can out-walk anybody here and maybe you too, but that's why you're guiding him. This Martin is a heavy hitter. He's makin' a name for himself as a real hunter and I'm lucky to have him huntin' with us. Just do your best and he'll do the rest."

And so it was when we tied our horses and headed out across the mountain afoot. Martin took the lead and kept it from the start. Now and then we would stop to glass this or that. Deer tracks made faint lines in the snow in all directions.

"How old is this snow?"

"I guess it came in good about five days ago," I answered.

"Are these deer stationary, or on the move?" he asked again in a quiet firmness.

"Well, they come in here from the high country from miles away. This is about the end of the line. They kind of stack up around here for breedin season and most of the winter. The does and fawns hang down closer to the alfalfa fields most of the time, but the big bucks seem to like it up here away from everything."

Martin grinned at my explanation and turned to press on. I wondered if he liked what I had just said, or was it that he was laughing at me? We marched side hill across the mountain through timbered draws and out in the open on once grassy slopes. Martin ignored the deer trails and even the beds of deer on the steep timbered pockets. We jumped deer from time to time and he ignored those too.

At lunch time I slowly explained that we sometimes sit by a migration trail and ambush the deer as they come by. Then too, a good vantage point looking over the bedding timber can produce at dusk when they get up to feed for the night. Martin agreed that these things work, but this day he just wanted to get a feel for the mountain.

I pointed to some draws that I had trapped cats and coyotes in each winter. I gestured toward the area where I had picked up a good many shed deer horns in the spring. I went on to tell him how the mountain got it's name and the names of the creeks that ran down from the rocky face.

Martin grinned again, "I guess you know how this mountain pretty good?"

"Yea, I guess I do," I replied almost defensively..

"That's good," was all he said as we got up from our rock and worked higher up before circling back to the horses.

Midday had warmed up some, and our continual march heated us up to the point of carrying our coats over our shoulders. The glare from the sunlit snow burned our faces red and we squinted without sunglasses, walking west toward the setting sun.

Back at the horses with about an hour of light left, Martin must have sensed by mood. We had seen several bucks, and even one good one, but hadn't attempted to hunt any. It had been a long day with nothing to show for it. Butch knew how good the hunting was up here, and I wondered what he might think of us not getting up on a deer all day. Day one of the five day hunt was ending fast.

"Okay Randy, I have a plan," Martin stated as I bridled the horses. "We will push six of these seven draws for the next two days. We'll leave the last draw for the deer to get used to as a safe place. After two days I should see at least most of the bucks living here and know what we have to work with. The one thing that could ruin the plan is hunting pressure from other hunters. What do you think?"

I pulled the cinches up and thought about it. I had never heard of anything like this, but it did make sense in some way. Even so mule deer were not whitetails, and moving mule deer around like cattle seldom works.

"Well, Butch will want to know what we're doin'. The other guides will hunt down by the alfalfa since there's a lot of deer down there. I guess we'll have the mountain to ourselves this late in the season.

"I'll talk to Butch. I'm having a good time, so don't worry about anything. We only have to find the biggest buck on the mountain, and we have four more days to do it." Martin sounded confident and slowly it was starting to rub off on me.

At 35 Martin was only five years my senior. Somehow he seemed vastly older. We hit the saddle and I led the way. Martin was not a horsebacker, deferring to me in at least this one area. My horse had a reputation as a bronc on occasion, so I hit him with my right spur just to show off a little. He flinched but didn't buck. Oh well, it was foolish anyhow.

We rode in silence down our tracks from the morning ride up. I felt a warm breeze against my cheek. A Chinook was coming in. It would be windy tomorrow, and I knew the deer would timber up tight to keep out of the wind. I thought more about Martin's plan. This guy had never laid eyes on this mountain before, but it just might work. The buck he would shoot at would have to be a great one, and that still worried me a bit. Guides sometimes measure their success on their hunter's success.

Martin broke the silence, "I see you carry a six shooter."

"Yea, I don't need a rifle when I'm guiding. It's just one more thing to carry. I might have to signal my hunter or finish off wounded game. If one of these horses would break a leg I'd hate to have to cut his throat." I was trying to sound pretty seasoned.

"Yea well, I had this guide in Idaho last year. He carried a six gun like most guides. I asked him about it too. He said he carried a side arm just in case his hunter would turn on him."

I locked up in the saddle. Martin chuckled. This was his dry sense of humor. He got me and he knew it. We were both wrung out from a day of hiking, but we were beginning to get to know each other. We hit the corrals at dark and the lit windows from the house reminded me of supper and the warm fireplace inside.

By the time I had put up the horses and cleaned up at the bunkhouse everyone had finished supper. Butch, the other guides, and the hunters were all having a drink around the fireplace. In hunting camp everyone seemed to drink whiskey. It was a tradition. Now and then someone might drink beer, but whiskey and Wyoming were almost the same right down to the spelling. Martin sat off to one side sipping brandy out of one of those big glasses with a stem on it. He's swirl it around and take a sip. He was hard to figure. I don't think the word "yuppie" had been coined yet, but Martin would qualify today.

Two hunters had scored on good bucks that day. They told their stories as their guides would nod to back up the truth. Everyone was having a grand old time, and we filed out to the barn to have a look at these two bucks. Both bucks hung upside down in the barn. Each had four points to a side and one had brow tines. They were nice heavy black horned bucks, the kind anyone would like to have.

Butch fire up the little wood stove while one of the guides went back to the house to retrieve the whiskey bottles. Except for the hunters, we all knew what came next. I was the official camp skinner. I prided myself in my skinning abilities having trapped fur since my boyhood, skinning thousands of critters along the way. I wasn't the best horsebacker in the outfit, Tom was. I wasn't the best packer either, Tom's brother Lou was. I was the best skinner though, and we all liked the set up. We kind of made a party of it, turning on the radio and throwing wood in the stove.

In reality Butch was a pretty good skinner in his own right, but seldom showed it. He was in his 60s and gladly allowed someone else the chore. I watched him skin an elk once and he impressed me with his speed. He joked that as a boy you learned to skin beef really quick when it wasn't yours to skin. At least I think he was joking.

I caped both animals for mounting and peeled the rest of the hides as well. The bottles were almost empty from being passed around, and everyone was considering a night's sleep. I resharpened my knife for the next time.

"Hey, you're pretty good at that," Martin kind of whispered as we headed for the house.

"Well thanks," was all I could say. Finally, I felt some relief in the presence of my hunter. I liked this guy. He had a certain way about him.

We attacked the mountain at dawn. I ran the timbered fingers while Martin would station himself at a vantage point, not to shot at anything, but simply to classify the bucks that would run out. In a while I got used to it. It was like some kind of biological study or something. The Game and Fish could even hire us to do this all over the place to get a good count on the herd. Martin kept notes too. This guy was something.

We finished our task by two in the afternoon. We had counted 13 bucks. Four were good ones. One was real good. I wanted to hunt him the rest of the day but Martin was sticking to his census taking plan. Still, no other hunters showed up to foil our efforts.

"Let's go back to the ranch and let these deer settle down. Most of 'em headed for the last draw and that's what we want."

"Martin, we can't go back yet. Butch will throw a fit if I come in early without a buck. He expects a full days work."

"I'll talk to Butch. Things are going just how I want them to go. Besides you already have put in a full day . The others are just down there driving around in the pickup."

Martin was all right. He always had it covered. The snow was melting and the warm sun made me drowsy. We spotted some bighorn sheep and I suggested to Martin that he should apply for a sheep license. He thought about it, then simply stated that he was a deer hunter.

Day three was much the same, but with a new twist. Martin had me work slower in each timbered finger. I threw rocks down into each hiding place as to not allow any deer to go undetected. Martin kept notes, and this time we got 16 bucks up out of their beds. Two big ones were running together that we had not seen the day before. I assumed that they had just migrated in here from the night before. Martin agreed.

"If you're not going to shoot yet, why don't you leave your rifle back at the horses?" I joked.

Martin laughed, "You got a point all right. I just carry it to preclude any altercations between myself and my guide."

I shook my head. He got me again.

I had to admit the plan was working. Most of the deer were headed for the last draw, the one we were saving. Some of the bucks had been jumped from our first six draws two days in a row now. The weather was still warm and mud replaced snow making it difficult to hike on the side hills.

On the morning of day four we spotted another hunter sitting smack in the middle of our operation. Martin elected to push out all the draws again. He figured that we might discourage the other guy with all of our running around. He was right. The guy got on his horse and headed down country about ten in the morning. I had almost given up on actually hunting deer when Martin made a quiet announcement that we would hunt tonight.

We went back to the horses and Martin reviewed his inventory sheets. He said he would take one of the big bucks that ran together. He guessed him at 29 inches. We rode to a point just shy of the last draw, and tied up where the horses were hidden in a small patch of timber. The last draw. By now it seemed like the dream corral to me. A corral full of big bucks. I have been in this draw more times than I can remember over the years, but then it took on a new mystical look.

We had about an hour of sun left and another hour of daylight after that. Martin laid out the plan using a stick in the dirt to map out what lay before us.

"That other hunter may be back tomorrow. We gotta do it tonight. Randy, you go down the mountain to the bottom of the draw. Work your way halfway up so your parallel with the horses here. Sit out in the open on the opposite side of the draw so any deer in the country can see you. They won't come out that way if they can see you. Any deer bedded in the bottom half should move up to join the deer in the top half of the draw, there in the thick timber. They shouldn't be too spooked if you stop here. I'll be hidden farther up on this side. When they come out to feed most of them should be exposed about 200 yards from that rock. That's where I'll be. We'll wait until the last shooing light if we have to." Martin's tone excited me. I tightened my boot laces for the trip down the mountain. This was it. Finally.

"Good luck, Martin."

He nodded slightly as though luck had nothing to do with any of this. I got the feeling that I was at least lucky enough to be in on some of the details. Down the mountain I went.

I picked a spot smack dab out in the open to sit down. It didn't feel right, but I did it anyway. I heard several deer move out in front of me on my hike halfway up the draw. The sun now slipped behind the mountains, and the breeze died away as it often does at this time of day. I could barely make out the horses in their hiding place 400 yards across from my position. I could make out Martin lying over the sloping rock. I had left my binoculars in the saddle bag in my haste to execute my part of the plan.

Two young bucks appeared uphill on my side. They spotted me and bounced, the way mule deer do, back into the timber. A small bunch of deer came out by Martin. From the size of their bodies I guessed them to be does and fawns. We were into the good time now. Deer were moving out to feed. It started getting gray and a chill replaced the warmth of daylight.

I spotted the white nose first. The white bridge of the nose is a dead give away identifying a mule deer buck. He stood still just inside the timber on Martin's side. I couldn't make out any more than that. I think I crossed my fingers, though I'm not sure. I never saw Martin move. His gun went off surprising me, and the sound of the shot echoed twice off the face of the mountain.

Slowly Martin stood up and in a nonchalant manner walked toward the timber motioning me to come on. I covered the distance in record time, winding up totally out of breath by the time I reached Martin and his buck. I couldn't believe it was so easy. Martin was right, he was 29 inches wide. He had four points on one side and five on the other, no brow tines. He had heavy black horns that really would remind some of elk antlers. This was a mature buck in the rut. His neck was swollen to the point that the deer's head looked too small for it's body.

"He's a good one Randy. I saw seven bucks in that timber and the does that came out here. Let's get some pictures before all of our light is gone. You go bring the horses up, and I'll set up the picture."

I dutifully obeyed, feeling pride in my friend and relief that this whole thing actually worked. I button holed the buck through the middle and Martin and I loaded him on my saddle horse fitting the button hole over the saddle horn. We tied the legs down solid and tied the head back around the cantle of the saddle to prevent it from flopping.

I was going to lead the horse afoot down to the ranch, but Martin wouldn't have it. He insisted I ride his horse while he led our deer laden horse back. Halfway down we stopped to make an adjustment of the load. I was tightening the cinch when Martin shoved two hundred dollar bills in my shirt pocket. Startled, I thanked him all over the place. In his way he just shrugged and said, "That's not for the deer. That's for the effort."

I'll never forget Martin and what I had learned. A little imagination can go a long ways in this hunting game. Outside the normal, or traditional methods there are a few, shall we say, "Tricks" that can work to your advantage. These are basically methods that are seldom employed however, invented out of necessity when the hunting gets tough.

Speaking of tough hunting, one should bear in mind that the old days are gone forever. Whether it is here in the U.S. or some far off African hunting ground, the easy hunting is over with few exceptions. Game has evolved to counter the challenge of more hunters in shrinking habitat. Mule deer are not stupid as many whitetail hunters might be led to believe. Black bears too, do not just stroll into the bait as anyone who has not hunted them over bait might think. You've got to admire these game species in their ability to adjust.

A long time friend and fellow guide and I have learned that our coyote howlers can accomplish more than simply locating coyotes. I have many times used my coyote howl to stop game in their tracks enabling the hunter to get a clean shot. My buddy Mike has used his howl to prompt a nocturnal black bear to come to the bait before dark. The bear responds to the call thinking the coyotes are eating his meal, thus he is attempting to guard what is his. The coyote sound is natural where coyotes are found and the howl means something different to different species of game.

Flagging in the hunter is another trick that works well in the right situation. If I have the right hunter, I might use the flagging method for a variety of stalks. I use two different colors of bandanas or handkerchiefs. One color represents the animal and the other color the hunter. I'll send the hunter off toward the animal he is stalking. He can look back at me to determine where the animal is against his own position by the way I hold the bandanas. This method allows the hunter to take short cuts, or realize the game has moved without him actually seeing it. If the attempt falls apart I wave both bandanas to signify the chase is over.

Some guides might use radios for this same purpose. It could be said that the use of radios is unsportsmanlike. I believe some states may even outlaw it. However I will not judge that here. I don't use them, but I have no particular gripe about it. People use bird dogs for birds, and many fishermen use high tech fish locators to find fish. These are aids that have come to be.

Radios can be valuable another way though. Guide and hunter can cruise the country searching for game. The outfitter can keep abreast of their progress by calling at specified times to see if they need to be picked up or resupplied. Perhaps the outfitter has spotted what the hunter is looking for somewhere else. Then the original plan can be changed for a better one.

It could be said that this communication might take something away from the wilderness experience, but it could also be that the radio could save someone's life should an accident occur in the backcountry. At the time of this writing cellular phones will not work in the country I work in. I suppose it is only a matter of time, but I can wait.

I'll credit the Montana elk guides with this as I know several who employ this trick on elk in tough country. Elk hunting is often times in country so thick with timber, and so steep are the mountains that getting near an elk seems impossible.

The right guide and hunter can climb to the top of a heavily timbered bedding area. If the guide can be sure of his elk, he will be positioned directly above the bed ground deep in the jungle of timber. Now hunter and guide will run at breakneck speed down the mountain toward the unseen elk. This means jumping logs and risking a bad fall.

The elk are caught astonished and flatfooted in their beds. The elk are not used to this tactic and don't suspect this type of assault. They may even assume it is another band of elk headed their way. Whatever the elk think, this method does work with some regularity. It is not a game for anyone with knee problems. In fact you could well develop knee problems playing this game. It is like I said, sometimes the hunting is tough and you have to turn it up a click to stay in the game.

I guess that since I do a good deal of guiding horseback I find that hand signals are very important. I would imagine that hunting from a drifting boat or canoe might be the same. Hand signals allow for quick communication without talking and giving away your position. My hunter, while horseback, is behind me just enough that whispering doesn't always get the point across.

Before we start hunting I clue the hunter in to my signals. When I motion my hand toward the ground with my palm down it means to get off his horse, get his rifle out of the scabbard, and move up in front of my horse. I see what we are after, and we better do something about this.

If I motion the hunter up to me with a slight wave forward it means that I have spotted something we should take note of. The hunter can simply ride up beside me and have a look for himself.

Now and then guides are required to guide several hunters at a time in pursuit of cow elk. Elk, when at ease in a herd, are very social animals having leaders and followers. If the herd is walking along it is plain that the lead cow is the one in front. If the elk are all out grazing it isn't as easy to spot her. If the situation presents itself it is wise to knock down the lead cow first. The others will generally mill about if they haven't spotted the hunters. This allows more time for a good shot at another cow for the next hunter. This is much better than flailing away at panicked animals for obvious reasons. Crow hunters and some goose hunters will tell you that the lead bird is the most important one to get first for similar reasons.

Decoys are an old trick for waterfowl of course. In recent years decoys have been used for predators like coyotes and foxes. Many have found, myself included, that antelope decoys produce results for getting that buck in close. It is true. I haven't had much success with the old flagging method for antelope, but I have had success using life-size three dimensional antelope decoys to get a buck into bow range. Elk hunters are even experimenting with various types of decoys when calling elk during the rut.

I use my horses as decoys of a different type. Sometimes I'll tie the horses purposely where game will see them. The horses will deflect game in my direction by sight or smell if I have played my cards right.

Not all hunting tricks are about bagging game. Some of the tricks used are ones that aid in the hunt overall. These are things to make life a little more bearable. Most of these can be read about in survival books, but here's a few I use.

In my pack frame or in my saddle bags I always carry an extra pair of warm socks. If you get wet feet, or the temperature drops it is no secret that this only makes sense. Socks can also be used as mittens if need be. Socks can be used as a pouch to protect your binoculars or spotting scope. Anything that needs to be placed in a container can usually be put in a sock. A sock can be fashioned into a bandage or can be used to clean and dry a wet rifle. Socks can be used as signal flags or a cushion to sit on. Socks weigh very little and take up hardly any room.

Fire starters come in many forms. Whatever type you like, take it with you. This little item can result in keeping the hunt fun in the worst of situations. I like those paraffin and sawdust sticks that are out there on the market.

Ask your guide if he has a first aid kit. He should. If he doesn't take yours with you. A modest little kit with the ordinary stuff doesn't take up much room. There will be a large kit in camp for the serious stuff.

In grizzly country the new bear sprays that are out could save your life in a grizzly attack. The spray might also save you a bunch of legal bills as opposed to the shooting of a grizzly in some places.

A small flashlight that fits into your pocket is important on any hunt. The ones that take the double A batteries are a good choice. Cold weather is hard on batteries. To avoid some of this carry the light in your shirt pocket. Your body heat will allow the batteries to remain warm and ready for use.

Try not to duplicate many items your guide might also have during the hunt. It is not necessary to carry two of everything up and down the mountain. Too many gadgets will only weigh you down and impede your progress. Hunters often come to camp with everything but the kitchen sink, only to leave it in camp after the first day of the hunt. A good outfitter will give you a list of things you need after you have booked the hunt.

"Tricks," for lack of a better term, are today's new way of doing things. Primitive people had their tricks. The lance, snare, bow and arrow became firearms and optics. Today's tricks will only be tomorrow's old fashioned way of doing things. I have faith that the sport will remain just that. The animals have been adapting with the help of seasons and bag limits. People become less skilled as new things make it easier on them. With any luck it will even itself out and hunting will remain hunting.

# Hunting Ethics
*Chapter IX*

Ethics. Every sport, even our lives has it's code of ethics. Ethics are those sometimes intangible rules that, if broken, are not necessarily illegal, but certainly looked down upon as unacceptable behavior. Good ethics are usually adopted by those involved in whatever it is we are doing. Hunting ethics have a long rich history to be sure. In fact, if enough hunters agree that something is unethical it is made to be illegal in most cases. "Fair chase" is the most common phrase heard when we speak of ethics.

Various societies, and or, regions have conflicting codes in the ethics department. Hunting deer with hounds is acceptable in some parts of our southern United States. In most areas it is illegal, or at least unethical. Subsistence hunters in third world regions may use poison tipped arrows. Most civilized hunters gasp at the thought.

Bow hunters may quietly agree that hunting with a scoped rifle isn't sporting. Rifle hunters sometimes conclude that bow hunting is to risky to insure a quick clean kill. The case of ethics runs the entire spectrum of possibilities of pros and cons concerning what is fair. On some things we reach a consensus. On others the jury is still out. So what is it we want?

It seems accurate to say we want to keep our sport sporting. By accomplishing this we can keep hunting honorable, while having fun at it. We can reap the additional benefit of keeping our critics, of which there is a never ending supply, at bay.

Hunting has so many variables to it that explaining it to the uninitiated is perplexing at best. It can be likened to explaining chess to someone who doesn't even speak your language. It's akin to anyone explaining computers to me.

By and large we hunters are satisfied to keep it "in house" so to speak. We are happy enough to sort it out ourselves, though when asked to do so, we have always delivered our own monies to keep our sport alive. And always means always. No other special interest group, if you want to call it that, can say the same.

Over the years I have been fortunate to guide world class hunters and those who saved years for their once in a lifetime guided hunt. Ethics has generally been the same with the working man, or the silver spoon crowd. On rare occasions have I witnessed poor ethics, though it has happened. In fact, I find myself guilty of this ethics business in the incident I will now let you in on.

It was a number of years ago. November 15 was the last day of deer season. My hunters had bagged their bucks and I had one day to hunt a deer for myself. I had turned the horses out the night before since my truck went in the shop for repairs. My only transportation was my little trapping truck, and hauling a horse trailer wasn't possible.

I headed up river before daylight. It was plenty cold and the snow depth was considerable even at lower elevations. I had been hiking after game since September and had a spot in mind where I could watch from the road for a passing buck. It was plain that I was taking the lazy way out.

I sat in the truck with the heater going as dawn gained some strength. The usual road hunters passed by. Each time another one came by I looked anywhere but where I expected to see deer. Even though I didn't consider myself a road hunter there was no denying the fact that that was exactly what I was doing.

Across the road and across the river the buck appeared. He stood watching the river deciding whether or not to cross. If he stayed true to the pattern I had watched other deer do, I knew he would. I slowly got out of the truck. I put a round into the chamber and waited for him to cross to my side. It would have been illegal to shoot from the vehicle or from the road. I would wait until he dropped from sight in the river bottom then make my move toward him using the river bank as cover.

As planned he dropped down into the river bed. I stalled out waiting for a car full of hunters to pass. They fell for my ploy of fumbling around aimlessly and passed by. With my rifle and lariat rope for dragging deer, I moved in and waited behind a small cedar bush. I waited, but no buck appeared. Could he have gone downstream looking for a better place to cross/ With my rifle at port arms I peeked over the edge.

At first glance I didn't see him. Then a movement caught my attention. The buck was stuck in the river. The edges were frozen for about 20 feet from each bank. He was valiantly trying to come out on this side, but his hind legs were treading water as he tried to lift himself up onto the ice with his front legs. It wasn't working.

I ran down to him not sure of my next move. If I took a shot then I would lose him as he floated downstream. At the sight of my presense so close he should have swam downstream on his own, but he didn't. He struggled and tried that much harder to get out right there in front of me.

I leaned the rifle against some sagebrush and started shaking out a loop with my lariat. It would have been an easy catch. If I could haul him out, then what? He made the decision for me. With one mighty heave he came up onto the ice right in front of me. I threw down the rope and grabbed the rifle. He just made it to firm footing when I shamelessly leveled him in his tracks.

In the span of a few seconds I was going to haul him to safety, then in the blink of an eye I killed this deer in what might be called anything but a fair chase. At first the whole thing seemed like an exciting, even though bizarre event. As I dressed him though the reality of the facts set in slowly.

I had broken no laws, but I knew what I had done. I was no stranger to killing, but this wasn't setting well. Another hunter stopped and came down to help me drag the buck back to the road. I told him the story. He didn't seem to be offended, though he kind of looked like he didn't believe any of it.

I still see that buck from time to time. I guess I'll always see him. That is the curse. To bag game at any cost can catch up with one in more ways than you might think. It has been said that "he who hesitates is lost." It has also been said that "only fools rush in." I don't know how else to put it.

On another occasion, on the same river, I was checking some mink sets since my hunting was over for another season. The cow elk season was on, and there were a few hunters about that morning. Something caught my eye in the willows several yards away.

A cow elk, with a bullet wound through her middle, stood hiding, unable to run. After a few minutes I spotted a guy up on the ridge. He had hunter orange on and seemed to be looking around in the snow, his head bent toward the ground. I figured he had wounded this cow and was tracking her.

I hollered to him and waved my arms, but he was intent at looking around at the tracks I suppose. The rushing river and slight breeze probably prevented him from hearing me. I walked out onto a gravel bar and fired my .22 trapline revolver once into the air. The shot got his attention and I cupped my hands to my mouth trying to explain his elk was down here. He watched me for a moment then turned and ran back over the brow of the hill.

I figured he was taking an easier route down and would only be out of sight for a moment or so. I walked back to the sick cow and waited. No guy! I started up the ridge and finally got to where he stood the last time I saw him. The tracks told the story. He simply ran off. Gone.

I can't say this fellow wounded this cow, but here she stood. I worked my way back down to her. She wasn't about to heal up, and wouldn't die. There were no other hunters in sight. After some thought I dispatched her with my .22.

Right then and there I had broken the law, and more than one. I took a big game animal with an illegal caliber for this type of game. I took her without a license to boot. I dressed her out and propped her open to cool.

The game warden was cruising the highway doing what game wardens do. When I caught up with him I explained the story. I knew full well that violations of this type could result in me losing my guide's license. I wondered if I was doing the right thing.

He listened to it all and shrugged. He would look for the guy I saw and take care of the cow later. He told me to forget about any wrong doings since he agreed with my decision.

One should remember that this was a judgment call on his part and mine. He could have written me up. Then again, I could have simply walked off leaving the elk to linger. Ethics, once they become law, one way or the other, can get mighty sticky.

Seasons ago I guided a pleasant older gentleman for elk. I truly wish I could remember his name, though sadly enough, I have forgotten it. This was to be his last hunt. He had spent a lifetime hunting big game here in the U.S. and Canada. Now, as his eyesight grew weaker and his body frail, he decided this was the last time.

The gun he brought along was a family heirloom. It was a .45-90 carbine. I don't recall the make, and had to leaf through firearms books to help me remember. I would think, from the descriptions and pictures, it was a Model 1886 Winchester Carbine. In any event, the rifle appeared to be as old as the hills. The ammo even looked old. The solid lead rounds had tarnished brass and an ancient air about each shell.

I'll call him Ed. He said that as far as he knew no one in the family had used this rifle for game since his grandfather's time. Ed thought it would be fitting to end his own hunting career with this gun that he held dear. He had fired one round at home before leaving for the hunt.

In camp he allowed me to inspect the carbine. It was a little dry in the wood and rust pitted along the barrel, but it seemed relatively tight and serviceable. We determined that he should shoot a few rounds in camp so he and I knew what we could expect from the gun.

It took Ed a long time to line up the sights due to his poor eyesight. He fired two rounds from a rest at a target set at 60 yards. Both shots were high and to the right, not by much, but by a couple of inches or so. If we got fairly close I figured he could score on a bull. I asked if he might want to shoot some more, but he declined as he only had six or eight rounds left.

Ed was a great guy to be with in the mountains. He couldn't get around well, and we had to pass up some good country because of this. Even so we saw a few cows and one bull much too far away to do anything about. The days were spent with me making him instant coffee by the fire while I glassed. He in turn would educate me on the Great Depression.

You had to admire the guy. He had had a tough life and it didn't appear that it was any easier now in poor health. Looking at him and his rifle I hoped I could find a bull, but the deck was stacked against us.

The weather turned cold. Sleet and wind compounded the problems of steep mountain sides and smart elk. Ed shivered and stuck to it. I prayed for a miracle. We rode farther from camp, staying later each evening, thus getting back to camp later at night. I was juggling his condition against his desire to use that .45-90 on his last hunt.

We wound our horses through the thick timber and deadfalls to a point several hundred yards short of a little secret meadow in the timbered bowl. It was afternoon, and big snowflakes drifted straight down on this very gray day. I knew this was only the beginning of the storm. I built a big fire for Ed. I reasoned that I could keep him warm here in the afternoon. As evening came on I could let the fire burn down to coals and minimize the crackling sounds of the fire. There wasn't much I could do about the smoke smell in the air.

Leaving my hunter by the fire I sneaked off to the meadow to read the sign. Luckily a few elk had been using it the night before. Snow had started to lay on the ground, but it appeared that one track pushed into the soft earth could be that of a bull. Before heading back I rearranged a couple of logs near the edge of the meadow for a rest and blind.

We huddled by the fire as the snowfall became heavy. I never carry a watch and Ed didn't have one either. It was hard to guess what time it was. I knew the elk would come out and feed that evening, but with this storm it was hard to get a feel for the day. There was a chance too, that the elk might move early as animals often do before a storm.

If I got my hunter in position too soon he would become chilled and give up before the elk showed. If I waited too long the elk would already be in the meadow, and more than likely spook as we tried to set up on the edge. We discussed our options with Ed electing to go early and tough it out the best he could. It was his call.

By the time we set up on the edge, the meadow was four inches of white snow. I wrapped Ed in my rain slicker from the back of my saddle. That would help insulate him from the wet snow. In a while he was just a white blob behind the snow-covered logs.

When hunting, it seems nothing ever happens until it happens. Hours or days of nothing erupts into big excitement in the blink of an eye.

Ed whispered to me "My foot's going to sleep."

I saw the bull at the same instant, "There's a bull!"

"I said my foot's going to sleep," Ed repeated himself to get the point across.

"I said there's a bull," repeating myself for the same reason.

Finally Ed caught on. He spotted the bull on the other edge of the meadow and the elk took two steps out into the clear. He was covered in snow as we were. A good six point, but he had the back fork of his left antler broken off. I didn't care, and I doubted Ed could see that anyway. It seemed as though angels sang as the bull put his head down to feed. His back was covered in snow as was his neck. His face was buried almost up to his eyeballs in it as he searched underneath it for grass.

The old hunter aimed and aimed. He took another deep breath and aimed some more. I waited for the boom. This would be the only miracle that would happen to us. The hunt was about over.

Finally, without whispering, Ed just said, "Let him go." At the sound of the voice the bull lifted his head and locked up. I froze hoping we could salvage this somehow. The broken horned bull lifted his nose, threw his rack back over his shoulders, and trotted off into the timber. The snowflakes fell in silence. Ed stared at the empty meadow as did I.

"Well, that's that, Ed said in a tired voice. "I couldn't make him out too good in the sights. He had so much snow on him I couldn't tell what part of him I was holding on. Help me up."

Under the circumstances I could see how that was probably the case. I helped the old timer to his feet. He limped and I steadied him as he stomped some life back into his foot. We brushed the snow from each other's backs and stretched our stiff bodies.

"I could have let one go. But I just couldn't be sure... I just have to be sure before I shoot." He was apologizing to me, I guess. In a way it was sad to say the least.

"Don't worry about it Ed. He had a broken horn anyway." I tried to make light of it all.

I don't know which is more critical, knowing when to shoot, or knowing when not to shoot. The old hunter knew his limitations. He had hunted a bunch in his time and killing wasn't as paramount as his decision "not to shoot" proved. We made our way back to the horses.

We were wet and the old carbine was wet too. I remember that it looked shiny. It had probably been a hundred years since it had shined before. Ed is more than likely gone now. The Winchester is probably somewhere unable to tell the story of the old man who had the good taste to do the right thing.

Ethics are sometimes like a faint star you can barely see. You may have to look away, then look again to make it out. A rock under the water in a brook looks like it moves, but you know it is a rock, and it isn't moving at all.

There have been times while guiding hunters or hunting for myself that I found myself in the middle of a bunch of other hunters. What do you do? Do you slug it out in a manner of speaking and compete for the game? Do you walk away giving up your own hunting in the process? These are not easy questions to answer as situations vary. Here too, the ethics are at play adding another twist to a serene, but nonetheless complex sport.

If your hunting public lands your outfitter may have an area to hunt where he is the sole outfitter. That's fine if you keep in mind that he has sole commercial use. The local hunting public may still hunt the area as they are citizens on public lands. They are probably not involved in any commercial use, therefore, they may be hunting the same country as the guy who is paying for the hunt.

In the West there is generally enough land for everyone. Only every now and then does a perceived conflict arise. The outfitter is providing a service. He cannot sell you game. Okay, in rare exceptions on private land this may take place, but by and large a guided hunt is just that. A hunt. So where do the ethics come in?

I have never shot a game animal out from under someone else. I don't know any guides who have. I'm sure it has happened, but I haven't seen it. I have heard sour grapes from guys who couldn't get out of bed early enough. I have listened to the fellow who came along as they were dressing out his elk, though he was only halfway up the mountain when the kill took place.

If someone is in your spot first it is generally best to move on. If you recall Martin and I pushed out the timber pockets while another hunter sat by on watch. I don't know if this was right or wrong. He was there first. It was mid-morning and no deer were moving. We had several days invested already in this spot. My efforts at rousting the deer could have resulted in the stranger killing a buck. What would have stopped him from hunting the one draw we were saving? On any given day I might do things differently each time. I don't know. I just try to do the best I can with each circumstance.

I have deferred to other hunters plenty of times. It is not only courteous, but makes sense to look for fresh country when you can. If a guide has a hot spot, it seems it lasts only until he is pushed out of it by others who have figured it out. Then it is time to find another hot spot. In remote areas this question of ethics is seldom tested. Within a mile of the road it happens. In the old days this problem of, "who is hunting where," didn't come up much. Today we have more hunters hunting less ground in shorter seasons. It is a fact of life.

Guides have another question of ethics that their hunters seldom recognize. It goes like this.

Guide and hunter are sitting on the ridge enjoying their lunch. After a few days of hunting they have become friends. This is a good and natural occurrence. The hunter may ask his guide, "Who is the best outfitter for deer? Who is the best outfitter for moose, etc., etc.?"

Well, those are legitimate questions, but think about it. The guide is working for the outfitter who this hunter is hunting with. The guide owes some, if not all of his loyalty, to the guy he is working for. The guide may in fact know of a certain outfitter who specializes in this or that, but he is reluctant to send his boss' clients off to someone else. If the guide says nothing he may appear to be less than informed about his own livelihood.

If a hunter has a question of a business nature, he should ask the outfitter himself. This is the best way to handle it.

Most guides love to hunt, and that is the foremost reason they become guides. Because of the work load however, guides may not have the opportunity to hunt for themselves as often as they would like. The question of a guide hunting for himself while he is working comes up only rarely. Professional guides are just that. They know what is expected of them. I have felt for a long time that there is plenty of work involved in guiding one or two hunters at a time. Even if the hunter should offer to loan me his rifle, another downed animal uses up time and effort that should be applied to the client. There may be rare exceptions to this of course, but here again the ethics of guiding dictates certain unwritten rules.

The fall of '82 was a dry one early on. We had a party of deer hunters out, and the hunting was tough. By the second day no one had fired a shot at a buck. It was a good berry year that year though, and there was a fair number of black bears working the berries. I was guiding a fellow from New Jersey.

At dawn of the third morning we were about to cross the river when my hunter whispered, "Bear!" I turned in the saddle and he pointed to the thick berry bushes to the right.

"He went right into those bushes just before you turned around, Randy."

"Did he looked spooked?" I whispered back.

"Hell no, he didn't even see us."

I love to hunt bears, but I didn't have a rifle. Besides it was getting light and I wanted to get to some deer country while the deer might still be out and feeding. My deer hunter didn't have a bear license, so I figured that was that.

My hunter leaned forward in his saddle and whispered again, "Do you have a license?"

I did have a license, but I wasn't about to let the hunter shoot something on my license. I didn't answer him, though I must have nodded in the affirmative because he shoved his rifle at me.

"Go ahead and get him. Go ahead."

I traded him the rifle for my reins. I sneaked down toward the bushes with the gun up. I figured the bear would come boiling out of there at any moment. To my surprise I spotted the bear eating berries right off their stems not 40 yards away. With all of this going on he placidly dined as if we weren't even in the country. One shot was all it took.

"I got him!"

"You did?"

"Yea, tie up the horses and come down."

We were both pleased over my chocolate colored bear. He had a fine pelt and was as fat as a butterball from all the fall berries. I tagged the bear and we rolled him in under the bushes to keep the sun off him. Remembering my responsibilities I figured we better get back to deer hunting. We would come back later to skin him and get the hide to the ranch.

We saw no deer, but we did see another black bear. At this point my hunter was bound and determined to run to town to get a bear license. He had never killed a bear, and this sure looked more exciting than hunting invisible deer.

All the deer hunters went to town for bear licenses. The outfitter, my boss, wasn't all that pleased with this either. The only saving grace was that the deer hunting was poor, and this sudden bear fever might turn a luckless hunt into something else.

My hunter shot at another bear and missed. One of the other guides found a nice all black black bear for his hunter and they scored. Nobody was even talking about deer by the time the hunt was over. They were happy hunters, but criticized my boss about not telling them early on about the great bear hunting. The five day deer/bear hunt ended with mixed emotions.

In parts of Montana and Wyoming, free ranging buffalo roam outside Yellowstone National Park. John James Audubon called them bison, and that is zoologically correct. Jim Bridger and the boys called them "buffalo," and it stuck, thus putting the "buffalo" in Buffalo Bill.

Hunting seasons for these buffalo takes place in an "on again, off again" manner as overpopulation and politics dictates. While guiding hunters for other game we often see buffalo along the road grazing like so many domestic cattle. It is interesting to hear the comments from the various hunters on the subject of hunting buffalo. This question again goes back to ethics.

The big shaggy giants aren't wary to say the least. Being protected within the park, the ones that come out searching new grass will stand well within camera range and fear nothing. They are dangerous if molested as an unthinking and battered tourist might admit. Still, today's buffalo might best be omitted from the sporting game list.

I must say however, that buffalo meat is much better tasting than some other types of game, and there is a pile of meat on a buffalo. Winter prime hides are beautiful to behold and the bleached skull or mounted head looks as good as most other heads on the wall.

Some hunters look at the buffalo and state that they can't see why anyone would want to shoot one. Others would jump at the chance to hunt a buffalo. Who's right? Who's to say who's right?

It is a matter of one's personal taste, and what each hunter expects of hunting. I'm using the buffalo as an example, although we see hunters comparing the hunting of this versus that all the time. A mountain lion up a tree may not seem as sporting as an antelope at several hundred yards, but one might consider what is only on the surface before he passes judgment. We hunt because we love it.

We hunt by a set of legal rules, and we hunt more importantly on the standards we set for ourselves. Ethics allow us to romanticize our sport because there is honor in it. There is honor in it because there are ethics.

*One of the most ethical hunters I have had the pleasure of guiding.*

*Grizzly with a kill*

# Dangerous Game
*Chapter X*

Sometimes things just happen. In grizzly country trouble is hardly a routine, but it happens often enough to keep you on your toes. Grizzly bears are grizzly bears in the lower 48, Alaska and Canada. A grizzly may charge you with intent to kill. He may bluff, charging right up to you and stop short of mauling you, or he may run from you like a scalded dog. In any case, this bear is unpredictable at best and I consider them, as do most guides, dangerous always.

It was 4:30 a.m. Rainwater poured down the side walls of the tent in the morning blackness. The deafening pelting of the downpour was at times punctuated by a blue flash of lightening and subsequent crashing of thunder. And so it was, the beginning of another day at the office.

The thunder boomer had about passed as I saddled our wet and shivering horses for the day's elk hunt. It was nice to see the stars come out, knowing the sun would not be far behind. I had to coax my hunter into the saddle, as neither one of us felt much like heading out into that cold dampness.

We rode hunched up in silence with large drops of water falling on us from the branches overhead. The trail wound through the black timber with no moon, but a little starlight to see by. On a steep sidehill the trail cut across the middle of a small opening in the trees. The mountain fell off sharply to our left, and was equally as steep uphill to our right. My horse hit the meadow first as I was in the lead, and that was when I heard it.

At first it was a low grumble coming from the other side of the opening, then a sharp cough. A slight breeze blew from my back toward the trail in front of us. That's why the horses didn't smell it. Another kind of grunt, then another sharp cough. I jammed the bit back, skidding my horse to a stop in the mud. Grizzly!

The bear was warning us, and I knew it. A sow may be guarding her cubs. A bear might also guard a kill, or a grizzly may just want the trail bad enough to kick you off of it. It was time for some fast thinking and I wasn't doing so good. I really expected to hear the bear go crashing off down the mountain. A man that is mounted generally has little to worry about since the size of the horses and man smell usually intimidates the bear. Instead he let go with another growl, this time followed by the popping of teeth.

I think Larry knew even before he asked, "What is it?"

"Grizzly, he's right on the trail in front of us. Turn your horse around," I whispered in a loud way.

The bear answered our conversation with some more of his own growls, and this time he pounded his feet on the ground for good measure. I spun my horse around to get out of there, knowing I would be covering Larry's backside on the way out. My horse plowed right into Larry's horse head on.

"Turn him around and get back down the trail," I was more emphatic this time though. I didn't want to panic my hunter.

"I can't, he won't turn, dammit!"

In the dark we couldn't see each other, but I figured Larry was trying to neck rein his horse around when he should have just grabbed a short rein and plow reined the old pony around. There was no time to explain. I ran my horse into Larry's and punched his old dude horse in the nose to force the issue. The old horse locked up in his tracks with my horse getting his head and neck right into Larry's lap.

The grizzly must have moved toward us, or perhaps the wind changed allowing my horse to now smell the bear. My horse seemed like he was trying to crawl right over top of the other horse. I pulled him back not wanting to knock Larry off down the mountain. It was steep enough that a rolling horse would be far more dangerous than the bear.

Larry was in a bind. The next thing I knew his flashlight was shining in my eyes blinding me and my horse. One doesn't have much vision at night, but a flashlight beam in the eyes robs you of even that little you have. Evidently my horse shook his head and knocked the light out of Larry's hand. The handlight rolled clattering down the mountain still shining.

At times like this things are happening so quickly that in relating the story it is not easy to explain the events in rapid order as it happened. We were in trouble. An angry grizzly is bad enough. Compound that with almost total darkness and bolting horses, throw in a steep mountain side, and you have a real honest to goodness wreck on your hands.

At last I was able to back my horse off Larry and pull along side of him. I groped for his lead rope in an effort to pull him and his horse to safety. Instead of getting the rope I came up with his rifle. Later Larry said he pulled the rifle from the scabbard to defend himself against the bear. I slammed the rifle into my lap and got the rope. I dallied around the saddlehorn and started straight up the mountain, pulling Larry and his horse up behind me. I heard brush cracking off to my left and assumed the grizzly was coming up with us. I dug the spurs in for more power, and we climbed higher through the thick timber. The pine bows would hit me in the face then bend back and hit Larry with more force.

My horse caved in, sides heaving, at about 100 yards up the mountain. We bailed off our mounts standing shoulder to shoulder, watching for the bear. Our knees knocked together like a couple of scared kids. Our jaded horses stood sideways on the slope shaking with exhaustion. I shoved Larry's rifle at him while drawing my pistol. Except for our noises all else was completely quiet. Lingering drops of water fell from the trees.

"I think he's gone," I finally said.

"How's come you took my rifles?" Larry asked in an accusing tone?

"I didn't mean to. Why didn't you turn that horse around?"

Neither one of us had any good answers. We both tried to do whatever we could think of at the time. We led our horses higher to a bench that flattened out giving us a place to tie up and get our wits about us. The sky through the tree tops was getting gray. We forgot about elk hunting while we sat on a log thinking our own thoughts.

In the fray I had lost the clip from Larry's semi automatic ought six. I went over to a spot where I could make out the clearing below. It was hard to believe how innocent it looked in the morning light. A pine squirrel chattered on and on down by the trail where just earlier all hell broke loose.

We hunted afoot higher yet on the mountain. Larry had another clip in his saddlebags. There were no elk there and we knew it. I guess we just wanted to give the bear time to leave and put the whole thing behind us. By ten in the morning we were even able to crack a few jokes about the incident. Bravely, we resolved to do this or that the next time. Our entire conversation now was Grizzly, Grizzly, Grizzly.

We led the horse back down toward the trail as it was our only way back to camp. Upon reaching the opening our senses were razor sharp, but the bear must have been long gone as the horses tugged at their leads for a bite of grass. We found the clip lying on the muddy trail along with a jumble of horse tracks and big bear tracks not 20 feet from our tracks. I couldn't find any cub tracks in the mud, nor could I see or smell anything dead that might have been a kill. Two days later two brothers from another camp were attacked and mauled by a grizzly bear some three miles from our encounter. Again, there were no cubs or kill. The brothers got a shot off, but must have missed as no bear blood could be found later. One of the brothers was hospitalized. The authorities closed that part of the country off for a few days hoping to find the bear, but they did not. Case closed.

Dangerous game is just that. You don't have to be hunting it. In fact, it might well be hunting you. Fang and claw, or hoofs and horns can be something other than trophies when you're in the wild. Our own life-styles today leave us with much duller senses than what we are really capable of. Some folks find it difficult to remain alert or "on guard" as it were, and I guess it's only natural in today's world.

Almost every guide I know in this part of the country has had his share of grizzly bear experiences. Two of my friends have been mauled, and several knocked down or treed. These occurrences aren't common, but if you are out there enough it could well be chalked up to the law of averages.

There is another aspect of dangerous game that is often overlooked in the action-packed stories that are told. The animal that may be attacking you might well be on the endangered species list or otherwise protected by law. Whether it be a rhino in Africa, or again the grizzly bear in the lower 48, the law frowns on the killing of protected animals. The results of killing a protected animal can involve embarrassing investigations that puts everyone in camp under scrutiny by the local officials as well as the feds. A happy hunt can be ruined as travel plans must be changed and all else suspended until the law can determine whether it was justifiable or simply an overexcited case of itchy finger.

If it is found that a hunter or guide has killed an animal in something other than self defense, his name appears in all the papers. He will pay healthy fines, lose hunting privileges even in his home state, or guide's license. At this point dangerous game is still attacking long after it is dead.

Most guides I know get a sick feeling in the pit of the stomach when a hunter shows up and declares that he will kill any grizzly that gets in his way. Outfitters and guides are well aware of the laws and the trouble this could bring down on everyone's head.

On the other side of the coin, is it possible that the powers that be care more about the animal's life than yours? Well, I don't want to get political here, but the law looks at it like this. You are the human in these situations, and as a human you should know the difference between right and wrong. Don't figure that the burden of proof is on anyone other than yourself after the fact. I don't like this kind of talk and neither may you. Nevertheless, it is a reality of the times.

This legal stuff could also be your undoing if it causes you to hesitate at the last second. If the seed is in the back of your mind that you could wind up in trouble by shooting at an attacking animal, you may wait too long and wind up in the hospital or worse. This dilemma is always at hand where dangerous/protected animals are found. There is no good answer as every instance is different, but there is something that may help.

Today's list of equipment to carry includes bear spray. This is an aerosol can with a trigger that when sprayed into a bear's face, should stop him in his tracks. It is the same principal as the use of mace on attacking human aggressors. The pepper spray causes immediate burning irritation to the eyes and nose. This spray will temporarily cause blindness and difficult breathing for the bear, sending him the other way in a hurry. It may work on other animals as well, but various brands on the market are primarily advertised to counter bear attacks.

The stuff does work, believe it or not. I have even used it to keep a bear well back though he was out of range and not charging. A fog of this spray shot into the air can be detected by the bear well out of the 20 foot range. If the bear is coming toward you slowly he'll get the point long before he gets there unless the wind is blowing the wrong way. It is the same as warning shots fired in the air or into the ground. If there is time, it is a good move.

It is not easy to put your faith into a spray can as opposed to firepower when some large animal wants to bite you or gore you, but upon talking with your outfitter, you will find that most of them will recommend that you carry the spray in addition to your rifle. Here again, in many places it is illegal to carry a firearm while bow hunting. The spray, however, is legal and might save your life.

Bears aren't the only animals that can become dangerous at the drop of a hat. Moose too, can become quite troublesome at times. Bull moose or cow moose charge people with enough regularity that they need to be given some respect. A bull in the rut, or a cow with a calf is capable of doing serious injury. I have often been of the opinion that a moose is too dumb to change its mind. If it is going to charge it probably isn't a bluff. If it is going to run away it may go miles before it stops. When a moose makes a move it will most likely be for keeps.

I was guiding my father on a sheep hunt in October. It was Indian summer with cool frosty nights and warm sun-soaked days. We cruised around the country with a little string of horses searching for the right ram. Aside from a few small rams and ewes, we hadn't found what we were looking for, but we were in no hurry as this was early in the 10 day hunt.

We were camped at the bottom end of an old avalanche shute. Some years prior to this an avalanche of snow had come down the mountain with such force as to take out all the timber and pile it up like large toothpicks in the creek bottom. Small pines from two-foot tall to six-foot grew in the slot regenerating the forest to its previous state.

It was midday and I had the horses picketed on grass while I cooked us up some lunch. Dad had decided to walk up the shute a ways to get a better view of the opposite mountain side. He carried my rifle with him out of habit, I guess, since there weren't any sheep near camp.

I was involved in my cooking chores when he hollered down for me.

"Hey, come up here and bring the camera."

"Why? I'm right in the middle of fix'n this lunch."

"Just come up. There's a moose up here and I want to get a picture of him."

After removing the pots from the little two burner stove, I shut off the propane and rummaged around for the 35mm. I hung the camera around my neck and hiked uphill to where I could see Dad standing by the edge of the timber.

"There's a bull moose right in here. Get in there closer, and try to get a picture."

He was right. The bull was standing in the shadows just inside the timber. I soon noticed that he had two cows with him. I worked my way around a few of the small pines and snapped a couple of pictures, but I knew the shadows were going to prevent a good shot from that angle. The bull was a good one. He had nice spread and decent palms. The bull was in the rut, I knew, but he seemed docile enough.

The bull made a chortling sound almost like that of a frog. I had heard them do this before while rutting along with their grunts and moans. The cows stood back well behind the bull, and Dad was slightly downhill from me while I eased around a tree to get a better shot. Yes, this was a mistake.

The bull waggled his horns once then came on, and quick. He came at me full tilt with his head high at first. When he got to the edge of the timber he dropped his head down. I'll never forget how the little pine trees just laid right down to the ground as his head swept them under, one after the other.

I jumped sideways behind a fair-sized tree just as the bull passed by me. He angled down the slope than stopped to lift his head around to see where I had gone. It was quite a sight, but now I was worried about him charging Dad who was still out in the open.

"Boy that was close. Don't move Dad. I think he's done," I was kind of giddy with adrenaline, and thought the whole thing was a little comical.

Wrong again. The moose got his bearings on me while I was talking and was coming back for another stab at me. He came full bore too, looking even more determined. All the humor of the moment was rapidly disappearing. I knew better than this, but it was happening anyway.

I ducked behind the tree and crouched down. It worked the first time after all. Instead of blowing right on by, this time the moose came around that tree fast and sharp like a barrel racing horse. For an instant I was eyeball to eyeball with him before spinning to run. I was in a crouched position and upon turning to run I found I couldn't take the time to stand upright. I ran with my fingertips clawing at the ground and running like a crab. The camera hung from my neck, banging off the earth at every turn.

We went around that tree trunk time after time. I couldn't believe this was happening, but this doubting attitude didn't change the fact that it was. That bull moose had his inside horn cocked low to the ground so he could get around that tree even better. I wanted to stand and run, but the moose was too close on my heels, and I was losing ground. I could feel it.

I don't really know when he quit the chase. He ran back to check on his cows, and I may have gone around that tree one or two times more before realizing I could stop. Dad was right next to me as I stood up.

"Boy, I thought you were a goner. His horns weren't two foot from that Wrangler patch on your jeans."

I was breathing too heavy to answer, and nodded instead.

"I had the cross hairs on him every time you came around, but I didn't want to shoot until I had to," Dad explained while I kept an eye on our friend.

We backed away slowly trying our best to keep whatever trees were handy between us and the moose. The bull seemed content to stay with his cows as we made our way back down to camp. The last thing I wanted was to have this bull getting into the middle of our string of picketed horses. The bull moose and his little harem kept to the upper reaches of the shute, and we kept to the bottom.

That night Dad and I rolled our sleeping bags out under the stars. We talked about the moose incident and counted the satellites moving across the night sky. Across the valley a giant rock slide gave way causing some alarm amongst the horses for a short time. Never a dull moment. I had a moose hunter booked and moose season was week away. I would get the pictures developed to show my hunter, and while falling asleep that night I knew I had a prime candidate for the hunt.

Two weeks later we packed in after the moose. I had a lady hunter and her boyfriend. We packed three horses for the trip, allowing three days for the hunt. All were agreed that this moose would be a fine trophy if we could find him again. They found my story interesting concerning this bull, though I got the feeling they didn't really consider moose to be dangerous.

It was a nine mile ride in to where I hoped to find our bull. At seven miles, we were riding through thick timber on a narrow trail when the bull appeared, standing directly in front of us on the trail. He had his same two cows behind him and had the same attitude as before. The bull challenged our pack string by shaking his horns and walking stiff-legged pacing back and forth. I knew it would be disaster if he charged us as there was nowhere to go in the heavy downfall and standing timber.

"Get off your horses, bring your rifle and come up here," I yelled back over the string of pack horses, knowing I wouldn't spook the moose.

They evidently didn't see the moose because of a bend in the trail. Becky and her boyfriend looked at me not understanding what all the fuss was about. The bull was puffed up and full of fight. He would look back at his cows then glare at us. I would have gladly turned the string around if I could.

"The moose is right here in front of me. Get up in front of my horse and kill him before he charges!"

They got off, Becky with the rifle and her boyfriend with the bullets. They weren't loaded yet as we were not actually hunting. We were simply riding to camp. Becky moved out in front of my horse and brought her rifle to bear just in time. The bull was grunting and convincing himself he could whip this whole outfit.

Three shots later it was all over. Becky's knees knocked together from the excitement of it all. Mine would have, but I had a horse between my legs. The bull moose was ours, and his cows slowly drifted back into the timber.

There are other bear and moose stories of course. I've had grizzlies running around in camp creating havoc when even gunfire wouldn't scare them away. I once had a cow moose get underneath my horse while I was on him, but dangerous game comes in other forms too.

Nick was guiding a hunter in the dead of winter searching the countryside for a good mountain lion. Nick had good hounds and several kills under his belt, but he was barely prepared for what happened that day.

Now and then you will run into a black bear guide or a lion guide that has been in on so many kills that he takes it for granted. Nick carried a .22 handgun as anything bigger was too much to carry. The hunter would be doing the shooting anyway if they treed a cat.

The hounds took the track of a big tom. The chase was a grand one as lion chases often are with the hounds baying and men running to keep up. The cat headed for a small creek bottom. Lion and hounds easily outdistanced Nick and his hunter, but as the pair worked their way toward the creek. They could hear the dogs barking treed.

This is what every lion hunter dreams of. A lion up a tree with the hounds bellowing below is the stuff calendar pictures are made of. The only thing was that the few trees that were there were small leafless cottonwoods and Nick could see no lion or dogs in sight, though he could hear them. The men ran on toward the sight and found an enormous brush pile covered with snow. The lion and the hounds were all underneath the brush carrying on in a real dog and cat fight.

All lion hunters seem to love their dogs more than their own families, and Nick was no exception. He knew what could happen to the dogs in the case of a ground fight. A lion can and will kill dogs in the blink of an eye. Both guide and hunter climbed up onto the brush pile hoping to get a glimpse of something down in the bowels of the slashings.

The fight heated up with one dog yelping from one end of the pile while the other dogs were barking from the opposite end. Every now and then a dog would run out from under the brush only to dive back into the ruckus from a different side. The hunters stomped the top of the brush much the way one would to jump rabbits out from under the brush. Nick was getting plenty worried and ordered his hunter to shoot the first patch of tan fur he saw. The dogs were blueticks, not resembling a lion in color, so that seemed safe enough.

Suddenly a head popped up out of the brush between Nick and the hunter. Both men swung toward it, the hunter with his rifle, and Nick with his little .22. The hound nearly had his head blown off, but both fellows held their fire realizing they were pulling down on a dog and aiming at each other. The dog burrowed back down into the fight. Nick saw the blood on his face.

"I gotta get down in there before he kills the dogs." Nick was at the end of his rope. He had to do something.

He laid on his belly hanging down into the brush. He crawled around in the snow to several points and peered in not finding anything, although the fight was going on directly under him. The hunter fell through with one leg up to his hip and he clambered back out quickly before he got it chewed off.

Nick was hanging upside down from the waist looking into the dark when a dog shot past him in a little tunnel sort of opening. He could see the dog huddled at the end of the tunnel facing back toward the other end. Slowly Nick's eyes adjusted to the dim light and he realized he was looking upside down into the face of the cat.

It took a moment for the gravity of the situation to sink in. The big yellow eyes were staring a hole right through him only a little more than an arms length away. The lion could reach out and grab him at any second. Nick wanted to call to the hunter, but any sudden shout or move could trigger the cat into an attack directly into his face.

With his left hand Nick held onto the brush to keep from falling head first into the hole. With his right he reached up for his revolver and brought it out slowly pointing it at the cat, knowing full well he would get only one shot. He had closets full of bigger guns at home, but they were doing him no good now.

Suddenly the dog at the other end of the tunnel decided he was up for more of the fight. Nick squeezed off before the dog could attack the cat again. At the crack of the pea shooter the bluetick tore into the lion and Nick heaved himself back up on top of the brush. The other two dogs heard the shot and popped out of their places only to jump down into the hole nearly knocking Nick back in in the process.

All hell broke loose.

"I think I got him! I couldn't wait. He was ready to take my head off!"

Guide and hunter stood looking down into the hole watching the dogs tearing at the dead cat. Nick ultimately reached down to pull the dogs out one by one while the hunter held onto his belt to aid him.

It was a big tom as toms go. He had a large square head and a prime winter pelt. The hunter was happy even under the circumstances. Nick carries a .44 mag. Now on all his lion hunts. The little .22 worked but he caught the lion perfectly between the eyes. An inch in any other direction would have meant a wounded lion in the worst of circumstances. Such is lion hunting and dangerous game.

The types of dangerous game we hunt varies widely in size and tenacity as we all know, but it is extremely important to be able to recognize what you're up against. The hunter must have a weapon with sufficient knock down power to do the job quickly. We have all heard the story about the farmer who uses a .22 single shot to kill a steer. We have also heard about the farmer who was slightly off in his aim, and said steer proceeds to tear up the farm in a wounded rage.

Your outfitter will suggest a range of calibers and bullet weights for the game you are to hunt. Take his advice. He is in the business of not only finding game for his clients, he is also in the business of bringing his clients back alive. If you don't own a heavy rifle you can borrow one perhaps, or in many cases, the outfitter will have one for you to use.

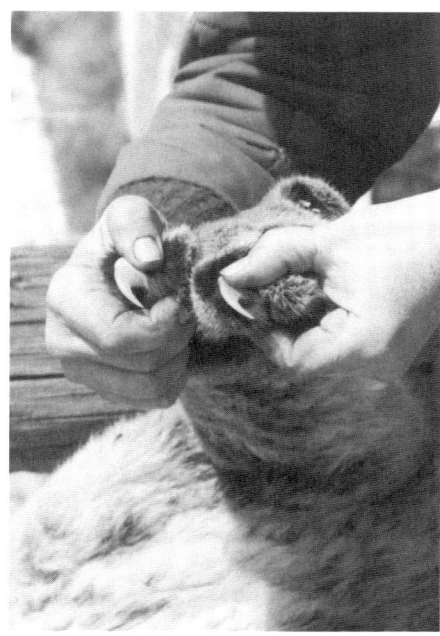

*The formidable claws of the Mountain Lion*

Guides too, take the threat of being eaten or beaten seriously enough that most guides carry sawed off 12 gauges loaded with buckshot or slugs. Bow hunters like the fact that although they may not carry a firearm in some places, their guide is permitted to. In this case the guide has a backup not present for a wounded deer, rather there for everyone's protection against some unforeseen attack by something larger.

I mentioned earlier in the book about shooting your gun before the hunt and how important it is to do this. If you're planning on hunting dangerous game this becomes doubly important for obvious reasons. The outfitter and guide may be watching you at your target practice session. They may be secretly evaluating you as to your abilities to get the job done. Don't be surprised. When you get to camp you will secretly evaluate them as well. This is only human nature. It is a good thing to determine everyone's abilities if it is at all possible.

I know a guide who guided his hunter to a bull elk a few years ago. The hunter knocked the bull down in a heap, and everything was going just how it was supposed to go. The guide and hunter walked up to the dead elk congratulating each other on their luck. As the guide moved closer to the elk the dead animal came back to life as quickly as he went down.

The bull came for the guide and had him pinned to the ground in short order. Luckily this fellow was small in stature. He curled up and was actually in between the bull's horns. The elk was pushing him around tearing up sod, a real deal. This, not so dangerous game, had now become an instant nightmare. The hunter had his rifle handy and waited for his chance at point-blank range.

Without much delay the hunter got a good shot off into the bull's boiler room putting him down for good. The guide would up with a few scuff marks but was otherwise no worse for wear. The moral is that in times of trouble it takes many things to get you through, but cool heads and teamwork will most always prevail.

All hunting has a certain element of danger. Not only are some of the animals we hunt dangerous to us by their nature, there are other factors that we take for granted when we shouldn't. Our own guns, and bows and arrows can do us in. Our vehicles might crash and our horses might buck us off. The mountain might fall on you, or you may fall off the mountain. Your own knife can cut you and your fire can burn you. The ice can break under your feet, or the hot sun can fry your brains. Is it dangerous game, or a dangerous game that will get you first? In reality the fact is that probably neither will get you. The fun is not knowing for sure.

I was packing a string of four young mules, not all that seasoned to the mountains. The horse I was riding was of the same caliber being a three-year-old, and although he was broke to ride he was now in the lead in strange country, to him at least.

The young gelding boogered at every other rock, log, and shadow. He bunched up underneath me at the sound of a squirrel or just some imaginary thing he thought he saw or heard. The little mules were tied together in a line gawking around at this and that occasionally taking a kick at one another. Seasoned stock goes down the trail in order and in a businesslike fashion, but they have to learn sometime.

I was packing fairly heavy with top packs on the mules in addition to the panniers. If one of the loads even looked like it would slip I would get off to fix it. I didn't want to risk having a mule blow up, thus setting off the whole string.

The sun beat down through the tree tops making a monotonous pattern of sunlit patches and shaded ones. My horse was confused by the light and dark places and unsure of himself, but he was slowly coming around. The miles and the afternoon drifted by with the sounds of steady travel.

The first one appeared directly on the trail 20 yards in front. The second one was off to my left only a few feet to the side of the trail, and not 10 feet ahead. Recognizing potential trouble I started to check my horse before he saw the danger. Too late.

Behind me, and off to my left, the first one let go and took to flight. The second one nearly beside me took off. The third grouse flew up from the trail in a heartbeat and the wreck was on. My horse tried to spin out from under me then commenced to buck. The mules all wrapped up instantly becoming a tangled mess. As my horse bucked down through the timber. The mules broke loose one by one and did the same, all headed in a different direction.

The three grouse were long gone but the wreck continued. I bailed out not wanting to get a stub of a limb stuck through my guts. The mules were having a contest of seeing who could buck off then drag their packs through the country in the most spectacular manner. I held my horse by the bit as I watched the mules come and go up and down the trail and all around. They weren't leaving the country which was good, if any of this can be termed as good. They were just having a stomping good time.

By the time it was over, only one mule failed to totally destroy his load. I guess he was the loser of the great contest. I caught them all with some cussing and coaxing, but what was left was scattered in all directions. Broken lanterns and ruined groceries were beyond repair. I swear it took two full hours to put it all back together again. I twisted my knee and took a good shot to the privates coming off my horse too.

The man eating grouse may well be the most dangerous and most frequent member of the dangerous game clan. Cowboys have Brahma bulls and grizzly bears on their belt buckles. I think the grouse is worthy of such display.